Collective Biography of Women in Britain, 1550–1900

Catharine Macaulay in her father's library, from Joseph Johnson, *Clever Girls of Our Time and How They Became Women*, 3rd edition, 1863

Collective Biography of Women in Britain, 1550–1900

A Select Annotated Bibliography

Sybil Oldfield

Mansell
London and New York

First published 1999 by
Mansell Publishing Limited, *A Cassell Imprint*
Wellington House, 125 Strand, London WC2R 0BB
370 Lexington Avenue, New York, NY 10017–6550

British Library Cataloguing-in-Publication Data
A catalogue record of this book is available from the British Library.

Library of Congress Cataloging-in-Publication Data
Oldfield, Sybil.
　　Collective biography of women in Britain, 1550–1990: a select
　annotated bibliography / Sybil Oldfield.
　　　p.　cm.
　　Includes index.
　　ISBN 0-7201-2321-6 (hardback)
　　1. Women—Biography—Bibliography　2. Women—Biography—History
　and criticism.　3. Women's studies—Britain—Biographical methods.
　I. Title.
　Z7963.B6053　1998
　016.9272–dc21　　　　　　　　　　　　　　　　　　　　　　　　　97–38287
　　　　　　　　　　　　　　　　　　　　　　　　　　　　　　　　　　　　CIP

Typeset by BookEns Ltd, Royston, Herts.
Printed and bound in Great Britain by The Cromwell Press, Trowbridge, Wiltshire.

Contents

Illustrations

OUR STORY

Let us now praise women
with feet glass slippers wouldn't fit;

not the patient, nor even embittered
ones who kept their place,

but awkward women, tenacious with truth,
whose elbows disposed of the impossible;

who split seams, who wouldn't wait,
take no, take sedatives;

who sang their own songs, went uninsured,
knew best what they were missing.

Our misfit foremothers are joining forces
underground, their dusts mingling

breast-bone with scapula, forehead
with forehead. Their steady mass

bursts locks; lends a springing foot
to our vaulting into enormous rooms.

From *Striking Distances* by Carole Satyamurti (Oxford University Press, 1994). Used by permission.

Introduction

Niemand ist tot solange man über ihn spricht
(So long as one is still being talked about, one is not dead)

Old Jewish saying

Already in 1929 Virginia Woolf articulated one part of the feminist historical project: 'We think back through our mothers if we are women.'(1) By 'mothers', it becomes clear, she meant mould-breaking foremothers. But where do we find such mothers? And who were the mould-breaking forerunners to whom they looked back, and the mould-breakers before them? One answer is suggested by the frontispiece to this book showing the historian Catharine Macaulay as a child reading in her father's library. Girls and women in earlier centuries read books by men about men and women. Some of them at least, like the members of every other culturally repressed and intellectually despised group, made an effort first to discover and then to transmit inspiring counter-examples to the depressing, reductive stereotype. As long ago as 64 BC, in China, for example, the first book of women's history was *Biographies of Several Thousand Women*. In 1869 the pioneer German feminist Luise Otto-Peters brought out her work of collective biography *Einflussreiche Frauen aus dem Volke* [Influential Women of the People]. In the late nineteenth century, the Arab women intellectuals Zainab Fawawaz and Maryam al-Nahhas catalogued selected biographies of Arab women pioneers going back to the early Islamic period.

In *The Origins of Patriarchy* (1986), Gerda Lerner's fierce and justified indictment of men for systematically excluding women, century after century, from society's institutions of knowledge, she attributes the failure of women to become intellectual system builders to their absence from history – especially from male intellectual history. Men have been able to build on the thought of men before them, whereas women, according to Gerda Lerner, have had to reinvent the wheel of women's history generation after generation. Women, in her view, have had to inhabit a mental world of temporal discontinuity – whereas men could live within history – a world that knew the concept of progress. While I agree with Gerda Lerner in deploring the absence of women from most men's idea of history, I am less convinced than she about the beneficence of intellectual 'system building'. Moreover, I believe that she has seriously underestimated women's persistent presence in that often naive but always influential mode of history – the collective biographies of Western Europe, most of them written by men. As far back as Plutarch's *Lives*, and his *On Virtuous Women*, c.100 AD on to accounts of the Early Christian Martyrs, the *Lives of the Female Saints*, Boccacio's *De Claris Mulieribus* (written 1375 – published 1473), Christine de Pisan's *City of Women* (c.1400) and Antoine Dufour's *Les Vies des Femmes Célèbres* (1509), it has been possible for women readers in Western Europe to learn about remarkable, mould-breaking women who were not content to live out their lives unquestioning, mute and confined either to the paternal or the marital home. Indeed, as Gerda Lerner herself has acknowledged in her *The Creation of Feminist Consciousness*:

> For centuries, we find in the works of literary women a pathetic, almost desperate search for Women's History, long before historical studies as such exist. Nineteenth-century female writers avidly read the work of eighteenth-century female novelists; over and over again they read the 'lives' of queens, abbesses, poets, learned women. Early 'compilers' searched the Bible and all historical sources to which they had access to create weighty tomes with female heroines.(2)

Precisely. Caroline Heilbrun in *Writing a Woman's Life* seems to me to have been quite wrong to suggest that:

> Biographers have largely ignored women as subjects ... Female biographers ... if they wrote about women, chose comfortable subjects, whose fame was thrust upon them [who] posed no threatening questions ... provided no disturbing models for the possible destinies of other women ... Only the female life of prime devotion to male destiny had been told before; for the young girl who wanted more from a female biography, there were, before 1970, few or no exemplars.(3)

This bibliography is a refutation of that view. A great many women have not been 'hidden from history' as orthodox feminist historiography has so often maintained. At the end of the twentieth century we may no longer know about the lives of all too many of our foremothers – but that does not mean that they did not know about theirs. However, what also emerges from this bibliography is that the collective biographers of women over the centuries, whether men or women, have not agreed about which women deserved to be remembered. Therefore this work covers three very different categories of collective biography – encyclopaedic collections of Great Lives, both male and female; collections of heterogeneous women's biography; and collective biographies of particular categories of women from saints to criminals – as well as many subdivisions within those broad headings, most of which relate to religious affiliation. The book is organized chronologically in order that a history of the collective biography of women produced in England before 1900 may begin to emerge.

It is clear that all the most significant encyclopaedic collective biographies 1550–1780 were compiled by male clerics who included very few women. Heterogeneous, women-only biography 1550–1770 consisted basically of men's listing of the names of great women who should not be forgotten. Mary Scott was the first woman to attempt such a listing herself in 1776. Collective biographies focusing on particular kinds of women – scholars, saints, witches, poets, actresses – had little historical or feminist content until George Ballard's *Memoirs of Several Ladies of Great Britain ... celebrated for their writing or skill in the learned languages, arts and sciences* in 1752. Ann Thicknesse was the first Englishwoman to compile a 'specialized' collective biography of women – her *Sketches of the Lives and Writings of the Ladies of France* (1780).

A statistical analysis of the first, most general category, Great Lives of Men and [a few] Women, reveals that the number of such collective biographies produced in the eighteenth century more than doubled the number produced in the seventeenth century; that the first half of the nineteenth century equalled the number produced in the whole of the eighteenth century, while the second half of the nineteenth century, even excluding the 66 volumes of the *Dictionary of National Biography*, nearly doubled the number produced between 1800 and 1850.

Regarding collections of women-only biography, both heterogeneous and special category, there were only a dozen in the seventeenth century and a dozen in the eighteenth century. That number doubled in the first half of the nineteenth century and then was six times greater again between 1850 and 1900. Clearly there was now a huge market for such collective biographies of women, a fact which may in part be explained by the new market in books for girls, especially as School and Sunday School Prizes. No fewer than a quarter of the collective biographies of women 1850–1900 were explicitly aimed at the girl reader, many of them written by Grub Street hacks.

In order to analyse the coverage of particular categories of women, the reader is directed to the Category Index at the back of this volume. In terms of historical period there were more entries under Tudor women, covering just one century, than there had been under mediaeval women over ten centuries; there were more entries under seventeenth-century women than Tudor women; many more eighteenth-century women than seventeenth-century and far more nineteenth-century than eighteenth-century.(4) In terms of religious affiliation, most biographical attention has been paid to Protestants – whether martyrs of the Reformation, Puritans, later Nonconformists of all kinds, or Victorian women missionaries. Catholic women had to wait nearly two hundred years after the Reformation before beginning to read their own counter-tradition of collective biography. As regards class, not surprisingly, royal and aristocratic women have had infinitely more individual attention paid them than the poor – unless they happened to be notorious criminals. In terms of chosen occupation, again Virginia Woolf was right: 'Writing was a reputable and harmless occupation ... No demand was made upon the family purse'.(5) Thus we find that 'writers miscellaneous' together with novelists, poets and playwrights constitute the most frequently mentioned occupation. Next come the actresses and singers, perhaps most enthusiastically remembered by their male devotees. Finally, in the late nineteenth century, women social reformers, educators and medical women begin to come into their own. More generally, what the Category Index demonstrates is the surprisingly wide range of categories for women before 1900. There are artists, composers, martyrs, political heroines, travellers and adventurers, as well as saints, 'witches' and learned women who were not to be forgotten.

As regards which works were feminist, either in intention or effect, I have marked with an asterisk all those authors whom I consider to have been affirming of women, aware of their cultural repression and eager to encourage their girl or women readers to think, to speak and to act for themselves. In statistical terms I consider there were a dozen such works – all written by men – between 1550 and 1780. In the 'revolutionary' period 1780 to 1830 there were another dozen, eight of them compiled by women. From 1830 to 1850 there were half a dozen, and that figure quintupled in the second half of the nineteenth century – both inspiring and accompanying the growth of feminist historical consciousness at that time.

What general interpretative conclusions dare I offer, however tentative?

I would suggest that practitioners, historiographers and theorists of women's history might do well to look much more closely at the range of collective biography of both men and women written by men before 1780 as well as at women-only collective biography written by men before 1900. What they will find there is both an astonishing array of mould-breaking foremothers and a surprising number of feminist male historians.

I would also recommend a more probing reading of non-feminist Victorian collective biography to which it is all too easy for a contemporary to condescend. Even when there is explicit adherence to Separate Spheres domestic ideology in a preface or a particular chapter, paying lip-service to the political correctness of that day, nineteenth-century collective biographers, whether male or female, may nevertheless still surprise a modern reader by their covert, subversive inclusion of independent minded women subjects practising alternative values and life paths.

In addition I would emphasize that, as with every other attempt at establishing a history, what one discovers in compiling collective biographies of women in England 1550–1900, is not one history but many different and even conflicting histories. If the woman reader had been Anglican she would not have learned of Dissenting or Catholic heroines; if Catholic, she would not have read the (dominant) tradition of Protestant women's biography. And within that broad category of Protestant, there were, of course, further exclusive subdivisions into Anglican, Calvinist, Methodist, Quaker and Unitarian biography – each very different and all enormously influential and inspiriting to their separate readerships. It is largely because so many of us, at the end of the twentieth century, no longer find it possible to be Christian, that we have lost touch with many of the heroines of our differently thinking 'mothers', for whom Christian faith had been central, 1550–1900.

So who were the women through whom our forebears thought back? Not surprisingly, it was the women who had been important in political history, that is, history that affected men, who constituted General Knowledge of Great Women: Cleopatra, Boadicea, Joan of Arc, Margaret of Anjou, Isabella of Castile, Catherine of Aragon, Anne Boleyn, Catherine Parr, Lady Jane Grey, Mary Tudor, Elizabeth I, Mary Queen of Scots, Queen Christina of Sweden, the Duchess of Marlborough, Flora MacDonald, the Empress Catherine II of Russia, Marie-Antoinette, Charlotte Corday, Mme Roland. These, together perhaps with Nell Gwynn, Sarah Siddons and Grace Darling were the women of whom 'every schoolgirl' had heard. But the frequency of appearance in the Names Index indicates rather more. A cultivated Englishwoman interested in discovering 'remarkable women' could, by the time of Jane Austen's death in 1817, hardly fail to know something of Anne Askew, Mary Astell, Mrs Barbauld, Aphra Behn, Elizabeth Carter, the Duchess of Newcastle, Susanna Centilevre, Hester Chapone, Susannah Cibber, Kitty Clive, Catherine Cockburn, Mrs Delany, Mary Wollstonecraft Godwin, Mrs Jordan, Catherine Macaulay, Mary de la Riviere Manley, Lady Mary Wortley Montagu, Nance Oldfield, Katherine Philips, Laetitia Pilkington, Elizabeth Rowe, Anna Maria van Schurman, Frances Sheridan, Charlotte Smith, Anne, Countess of Winchilsea and Peg Woffington.

By 1900, such a woman reader would also have discovered Jane Austen, Joanna Baillie, Barbara Bodichon, Rosa Bonheur, Frederika Bremer, Charlotte Brontë, Elizabeth Barrett Browning, Mary Carpenter, Anne Damer, Maria Edgeworth, George Eliot, Millicent Fawcett, Elizabeth Fry (*the* heroine of the nineteenth century), Margaret Fuller, Mrs Gaskell, Frances Ridley Havergal, Felicia Hemans, Caroline Herschel, Elizabeth Inchbald, Lucy Hutchinson, Anna Jameson, Swift's Stella, Angelica Kauffmann, L.E.L., Harriet Martineau, Mary Russell Mitford, Hannah More, Florence Nightingale, Caroline Norton, Amelia Opie, 'Sister Dora', Hester Thrale Piozzi, Rachel, Mme Viardot Garcia, Lady Rachel Russell, Elizabeth Smith, Mary Somerville, Mme de Stael, Lady Hester Stanhope, Harriet Beecher Stowe, Mme Vestris, Susanna Wesley and Charlotte Yonge. Through how many of these women can we still 'think back'? And whom did our foremothers not know – Mary Collier, Dorothy Wordsworth, Harriet Taylor, Sojourner Truth, Harriet Tubman, Eleanor Marx, Emily Dickinson? Or about whom did they know very little – Mary Shelley, Josephine Butler, Mary Ward?

Our own sceptical, ironic culture has little place for ancestor worship of any kind. Together with our loss of faith in God has come a loss of faith in humanity by the end of this century. The very concept of Exemplary Lives has come to seem not merely old-fashioned but dubious if not outright pernicious – concealing all manner of humbug. In part this is the fault of the Exemplary Lives genre. As Donald Stauffer so admirably put it:

> [The] polite school of biography ... [sprang] from the exemplary lives of [seventeenth century] clerics. Yet it became secularized, and dominated the theory of biography to such an extent that Carlyle in the nineteenth century still [cried] out in rabid wrath: 'How delicate, how decent is English biography, bless its mealy mouth!' ... The suppression of faults can easily lead to the suppression of peculiarities ... [The] study of eminent virtue includes only the typical, not individual, traits, for they alone are to be emulated.(6)

A film of dull, pietistic varnish covers all too many of the accounts of outstanding women listed in this bibliography, obscuring their real vitality and force of personality. One has only to compare the dullness of eighteenth- and nineteenth-century accounts of Lady Gethin, with the far more lively entry in Blain, Clements and Grundy (1990). Among the rare exceptions to the low literary level of this genre I would instance Foxe, Besse, Challoner, Shields, Louisa Costello, Julia Kavanagh, M. Betham-Edwards, Lina Eckenstein, and the contributors to the *DNB* – notably Jennet Humphreys who wrote 47 articles on women and Sir Sidney Lee's sister Elizabeth who wrote over a hundred.(7) Ultimately, the nineteenth century overdosed on hagiography and the inevitable reaction set in. Lytton Strachey, Freud, World War I, the sickening personality cults of mad twentieth-century dictators and the apparently ubiquitous corruption in high places in every nation, all have contributed their mite to our seeing only the feet of clay in our famous dead. Most recently, fashionable scepticism concerning 'the continuous self', the creative genius and the very possibility of disinterestedness have, together, dealt the final blows to the concept of Noble Lives. Our eager iconoclasm has only omitted to include the proponents of iconoclasm themselves. Irreverence towards our dead is something upon which we rather pride ourselves. 'With us, heroism is at a discount ... a symptom to be analysed rather than a virtue to be emulated.'(8) 'Much easier than your works/To sell your quirks', as the poet D. J. Enright noted in 'Biography'. Or, as Tim Hilton wrote of a recent exhibition in the National Portrait Gallery:

> Not a single artist in this show truly takes on the problem of grandeur. For good or ill, the idea that painting might accord great respect to an admirable human being has disappeared. Today's portraits are about fun, and they are shot through with irony and knowingness.(9)

There are, of course, pitfalls in Heroism. Not only may it involve untruthful idealization and hence the promotion of totally unrealistic models for emulation, but it also risks, through its focus on extraordinary individuals, ignorance of the lives of the ordinary, representative women in each generation. But do we have to choose between writing social history of the nameless millions and biography of those whose names have been recorded? I believe the risks entailed by No-Heroism to be still more damaging than the pitfalls of hagiography. Just as individual identity is inseparable from – and dependent upon – individual memory, so collective identity is inseparable from collective memory. And the collective memory of the socially subordinate, culturally disadvantaged majority of human beings known as women needs to accumulate positive examples in order for us to enlarge our ideas of what is humanly possible for women. Models of some kind we have to have in each generation. Madonna, Margaret Thatcher and Princess Diana are but poor substitutes for Anne Askew, Mary Ward, Mary Fisher, Elizabeth Gaunt, Susannah Cibber, Mrs Delany, Caroline Herschel, Elizabeth Fry, Catherine Wilkinson, Mary Carpenter or Agnes Jones. This bibliography is intended not only as a contribution to British historiography 1550–1900 but also as an aid and stimulus to further twenty-first century research in women's history. Then, when it is our granddaughters' turn to confront the venal and the inhumane in the decades to come, they will know that there were countless women of integrity, creativity and courageous sympathy before them. Thinking back through such 'mothers' should give them strength.

NOTES

1 Virginia Woolf, *A Room of One's Own*, Hogarth Press, London, 1929, p. 114. It is interesting that Virginia Woolf herself had only a very limited knowledge of the 'mothers' through whom her mother's 'mothers' had thought back.
2 Gerda Lerner, *The Creation of Patriarchy*, Oxford University Press, 1986, ch. 11, pp. 224–5. See also 'The Search for Women's History' in her *The Creation of Feminist Consciousness*, Oxford University Press, 1993.
3 Ballantine Books, New York, 1988, Introduction, pp. 21, 26. For another perspective on women biographers see Rohan Maitzen's interesting essay on Victorian women's historical biographies, 'This Feminine Preserve', focusing principally on their histories of queens and the contemptuous masculine reception, *Victorian Studies*, Spring 1995. See also Joan Thirsk's 'The History Women', *Historical Studies*, forthcoming.
4 See Virginia Woolf: 'How, then, does Affable Hawk account for the fact which stares me, and I should have thought any other impartial observer, in the face, that the seventeenth century produced more remarkable women than the sixteenth, the eighteenth than the seventeenth, and the nineteenth than all three put together?' 'The Intellectual Status of Women', *New Statesman*, 9 October 1920, Appendix III, *The Diary of Virginia Woolf*, vol. II.
5 'Professions for Women', 1930, first published in Virginia Woolf, *The Death of the Moth*, 1947.

6 *English Biography before 1700*, Oxford University Press, 1930 – 'A Critical Survey', pp. 250–2.
7 See Gillian Fenwick, *Women and the Dictionary of National Biography*, Scolar Press, 1994.
8 David Marquand, review of Clive Ponting's biography of Churchill, *Independent on Sunday*, 8 May 1994, p. 34. See also R. Skidelsky, 'Only Connect: Biography and Truth', in Homberger and Charmey, *The Troubled Face of Biography*, Macmillan, 1988; Ben Pimlott, 'Artists of the Lives–the future of political biography in an anti-heroic age', *The Independent on Sunday*, 14 August 1994.
9 'Farewell grandeur, hello fun', *The Independent on Sunday*, 21 November 1993. See also Madeleine Bunting: 'There is a curious late 20th Century obsession with destroying reputations ... as we metaphorically murder the figures who have framed our history and culture.' 'Prophet's Loss' in the *Guardian*, 13 August 1998.

Acknowledgements

This 'select' bibliography of the collective biography of women produced in Britain between 1550 and 1900, however incomplete, could not have been compiled without access to the stacks of the London Library, the immense helpfulness of the Interlibrary Loans staff of my own library at the University of Sussex and, of course, the resources of the British Library, especially the library of King George III.

Like all students of women's biography in Britain, I am very indebted to the work of Gillian Fenwick on the *Dictionary of National Biography* and especially to her volume on *Women and the DNB*, 1994. I am also grateful to Alison Booth of the University of Virginia, who is preparing a literary study of collective biography 1830–1940, for referring me to Rohan Maitzen's essay 'This Feminine Preserve', in *Victorian Studies*, Spring 1995, and to Jenny Uglow for her tour de force, the *Macmillan Dictionary of Women's Biography*.

The Bibliography

c.1559

1   Bercher, William. *The Nobylytte of Wymen.*

Mss. Not published till 1904 when edited with introduction and notes by R. W. Bond [and a preface by C. B. Morlay], 2 volumes, 1904, 1905. See London III, Roxburghe Club in BL.

Written by scholar of Magdalen College, focuses on sixteenth-century learned ladies, including Bercher's former patroness at Cambridge, Anne Boleyn, and Margaret Roper, Lady Jane Grey, Mary Tudor, Elizabeth I, the Howards, the Seymours, the Cookes, Lady Warwick.

See Doris Stenton, *The Englishwoman in History* (1957).

1563

2   *Foxe, John. *Acts and Monuments of these latter and perillous dayes, touching matters of the Church, wherein are comprehended and described the great persecutions and horrible troubles, that have been wrought and practised by the Romish prelates specially in this Realme of England and Scotlande, from the yeare of our Lorde, a thousande, unto the tyme now present. Gathered and collected according to the true copies and writings certificatories. Popularly known as The Book of Martyrs.*

John Day, London. Folio.

THE BURNING OF ROSE ALLIN'S HAND BY SIR EDMUND TYREL, AS SHE FETCHED WATER FOR HER SICK MOTHER.

1. The burning of Rose Allin's hand by Sir Edmund Tyrel, from Foxe's *Book of Martyrs*, 1563.

The impact of Foxe's account of religious persecution in England, especially under Mary Tudor, is impossible to exaggerate. New editions came out in 1570, 1576, 1583, 1596, 1610, 1632, 1641, 1684, 1761, 1776, 1782, 1784, 1785, 1795, 1807, 1811, 1817, 1822, 1824, 1837, 1838, 1839, 1841, 1843–9, 1848, 1863, 1865–7, 1868, 1870, 1871, 1872, 1877, 1877–9, 1881, 1886, 1888, 1894 and 1900. Abridgements and Extracts were published in 1573, 1589, 1598, 1615, 1641, 1645, 1660, 1676, 1688, 1741, 1746, 1747, 1761, 1807, 1812, 1816, 1819, 1830, 1837, 1839, 1846, 1848, 1851, 1853, 1855, 1859, 1869, 1870, 1871, 1873, 1880, 1890, and 1892. Too often Foxe's influence is reduced to little more than mere incitement to anti-Popery. Henry Kamen's *Rise of Toleration* (1967) places it instead as a humanist work essential to the evolution of religious toleration. Its importance for the development of feminist consciousness, however, has still not been sufficiently acknowledged. Foxe stressed that women were not protected from the barbarities of persecution:

> The bloody rage of this [Marian] persecution spared neither man, woman, nor child, wife, nor maid, lame, blind nor cripple; and ... as there was no difference either of sex or age considered, so neither was there condition or quality respected of any person, but whosoever he were, that held not as they did on the pope, and sacrament of the altar, were he learned or unlearned, wise or simple innocent, all went to the fire.

Foxe's martyrology covers, after the Early Christians and Lollards, those who had suffered within living memory in the mid-sixteenth century. He includes vivid, eye-witness accounts of the arrest, interrogation and execution of Rose Allin, Anne Askew, Margaret Austoo, Alice Bender, Joan Bocher, Katherine Cawcher, Elizabeth Cooper, Alice Driver, Margaret Ellis, Ellen Ewring, Elizabeth Folkes, Isabel Foster, Agnes George, Agnes Grebil, Margaret Hide, Joan Hornes, Catherine Hut, Alice Knight, Margaret Mearing, Margery Morice, Alice Mount, Cicely Ormes, Elizabeth Pepper, Margery Polley, Alice Potkins, Agnes Potten, Agnes Silverside, Joan Sole, Alice Snoth, Agnes Stanley, Elizabeth Thackrel, Margaret Thurston, Anne Tree, Elizabeth Warne, Joan Waste and Thomasin Wood, all of whom would have been read as inspirational resistance heroines against both state and church by young Protestant Englishwomen – especially nonconformists, century after century.

An essential, underused source for British women's history.

c.1610

3   Anon. *The Lives of Women Saints of our Contrie of England. Also Some Other Lives of Holie Women written by some of the Auncient Fathers.*

Mss. Stowe 949 by Roman Catholic theologian, not published till 1886, edited by C. Horstmann. See London English Text Society, BL.

Includes: Saints Brigid, Dympna, Ebba, Edith, Ethelburge, Hilda of Whitby, Mildred and Wenefrede. The second part includes St Monica, St Agnes, St Nonna, and St Macrina. Praises noble virgins and widows for renouncing carnal love: 'The weaker they were by nature, so much more admirable they were to excell the perfecter sex by grace ... But god's grace maketh little difference of sexe.' Their holiness was attested by their miracles, asceticism, charity, monasticism and otherworldly religious devotion.

1613

4   Potts, Thos. *The Wonderfull Discoverie of Witches in the Countie of Lancaster with the Arraignment and Triall of 19 notorious Witches, at the assizes and generall Gaole deliverie holden at the Castle of Lancaster, upon Monday 17th August 1612.*

Printed by W. Stansbury for John Barnes, dwelling neare Holborne Conduit, London.

Assumed guilty before and throughout their 'Triall', the Pendle 'Witches' included 80-year-old, decrepit and almost blind Anne Whittle. They, together with her mother and grandmother, were accused by 9-year-old Jennet Device of practising black magic. She had seen 'a Spirit come in the likeness of a Brown dog called Ball'. Anne Whittle, Alison Device, Elizabeth Device, Anne Readfearne, Alice Nutter, Katherine Hewytte, Jane Bulcocke, Isabell Robey and Margaret Pearson were all hanged.

1640

5   Heywood, Thos. *The Exemplary Lives and Memorable Acts of Nine of the Most Worthy Women of the World: three Jews, three Gentiles, three Christians.*

Published by T. Cotes for R. Royston, London.

Includes: Deborah, Judith and Esther; Boadicea, Penthesilea and Artemisia; Elpheda, daughter of Alfred, Queen Margaret and Queen Elizabeth I – 'a Vestall for Virginitie, to her friends a mother, her foes a terror'.

1646

6   Clark, Samuel. *A Mirrour or Looking Glasse both for Saints and Sinners: wherein by many memorable examples is set forth, as God's exceeding*

*great mercies to the one, so his severe judgements upon the other ...
collected out of the ancient fathers, eccles. writers, modern divines, the
Chronicles of severall countries, and other authors of good credit.*

Published by Ric. Cotes for John Bellamy, London.

Later editions 1654, 1657, 1671.

Gruesomely intolerant version of Puritanism; includes the 'hereticks'
Mistris Dyer of Boston and Mistris Hutchinson who held 'about
thirty monstrous and hereticall opinions and had thirty monstrous
births none of humane shape, before being abducted and killed by
Indians'.

1648

7   Stearne, John. *A Confirmation and Discovery of Witchcraft, containing these severall particulars That there are Witches called bad
Witches, and Witches untruely called good or white Witches, and what
manner of people they be, and how they may be knowne ... Together
with the Confessions of many of those executed since May 1645.*

William Wilson, Little St Bartholomew, nr Smithfield, London.

Stearne was the agent aiding Witch-finder Hopkins. This is his
unapologetic apology for identifying and prosecuting 'Devill-worship-
ping old women': 'the greatest Idolaters that can be and are not they
then more worthy of death? ... I desire to give some satisfaction to the
world, that it may appeare what hath been done hath beene for the
good of the commonwealth and we free from those aspersions cast
upon us. I never favored any or unjustly prosecuted others.'

Among the 200 suspects executed in Essex, Suffolk, Northampton-
shire, Huntingdonshire, Bedfordshire, Norfolk, Cambridgeshire and
the Isle of Ely, 'women farr [exceeded] the men in number ... beeing
more apt to revenge and thereby more fit instruments for the Devill'.
Among those tried and executed Stearne lists Elizabeth Deeke and
her mother, Joan Wallis, Elizabeth Fine, Thomazine Ratcliffe, Anne
Randall, Meribell Bedford, Elizabeth Hubbard, Alice Wright, Ellen
Greenlief, Anne Crick, Susan Scot, Anne Goodfellow, Elizabeth
Gurney and Anne Boreham. Many of them were widows on whose
bodies Stearne claimed to have found marks left by Satan's Imps.

1651

8   *Gerbier, Charles. *Elogium Heroinum or The Praise of Worthy
Women.**

London.

A praise-song to 'Woman, the miracle of the world, the marvel of marvels' dedicated to Elizabeth of Bohemia and several aristocratic English ladies. Chapter headings include 'Of the Wisdome and learning of some women', for example, Themistoclea, Aspasia, Hypatia, Christine de Pisan, Anna Maria van Schurman. 'Of women's abilities to govern – they have therein excelled most men ... this sex hath not [produced] such monsters as a Nero, Caligula, Sulla, Herod, Harius, Nimrod ... and a hundred such others.'

1652

9   Le Moyne, Peter S. J. *The Gallery of Heroick Women.*

London. Folio. Illustrated. Printed by R. Norton for Henry Seile over against St Dunstan's Church in Fleett.

Translated by the Marquess of Winchester, the Catholic monarchist defender of Basing House against Cromwell's battery – written in the Tower and printed at his own expense.

2. Joan of Arc sent by God to save France, from Le Moyne, *The Gallery of Heroick Women,* 1652. Courtesy of The Fawcett Library, London Guildhall University.

Translator's address to the Ladies of this Nation – 'this land of trial':
'These Gallant Heroesses repaired first from all the Regions of History
to lay down their Crowns at the Queen Regent's [Anne of Austria's]
Feet. ... The conversation of such brave women cannot chuse but be
most delightful and instructive to you ... chiefly those Christian
Heroesses.' He includes Deborah, Jahel, Judith, Salomona, Mariamne, Panthea, Camma, Artemisia, Monima, Zenobia, Lucretia,
Claelia, Portia, Arria, Pauline, Judith of Burgundy, Eleanor of Castile,
Joan of Arc, Isabella of Castile, Mary Stewart [sic] ('[Her] Tragedy is
not only Inhumane, but Monstrous. And yet England applauds.') The
presence of so many righteous political assassins raises the question of
whether this English translation might not have been meant to incite a
devout Catholic woman reader to kill Cromwell.

1662

10   Fuller, Thos., D. D. *The History of the Worthies of England.*

I.G.W.L., W.G. London. Folio.

Categorized under counties and listed chronologically, Fuller's few
'worthy' women include not only royal women but also the great
benefactresses of male learning: 'It is better to found schools than
monasteries.' He affirmed Anne Clifford for building a hospital 'in
this age, wherein so much was demolished' and praises scholarly

3. Lady Anne Clifford,
Countess of Dorset,
Pembroke and
Montgomery, from
Louisa Stuart Costello,
*Memoirs of Eminent
Englishwomen,* 1844–6.

women – St Hilda, Margaret Roper and Elizabethe Jane Weston. 'Here we may see how capable the weaker sex is of learning, if instructed therein.' Mary Waters of Kent is singled out both because of her 367 descendants and that in 'the days of Queen Mary she used to visit the prisons, to comfort and relieve the confessors there'.

1669

11   Aubrey, John. *Brief Lives.*

Mss. First published 1898, edited by Andrew Clark, 2 volumes. Clarendon Press, Oxford.

Chiefly Aubrey's contemporaries; women mentioned for the most part as scandalous, gossipy footnotes in the lives of his male subjects, for example, Venetia Stanley.

1671

12   Janeway, James. *A Token for Children, being an Exact Account of the Conversion, Holy and Exemplary Lives, and Joyful Deaths, of several young Children, Parts I and II.*

D. Newman, London. 1671–2. Later editions 1720, 1771, 1785, 1792, 1793, 1799, 1813, 1820, 1830, 1836, 1863.

A compilation of thirteen narratives including several girls.

Preface: 'O children, if you love me, if you love your Parents, if you love your Souls; if you would escape Hell fire and if you would live in Heaven when you dye, do you go and do as these good children.' 'One of the most powerful pieces of writing ever produced for children' Gillian Avery, in Avery and Briggs, *Children and their Books* (1989) and see Iona and Robert Opie and Brian Alderson's *The Treasures of Childhood* (1995) on its status as 'among the earliest of all English children's books'.

1672

13   Janeway, James. *A Token for Youth. Containing the Lives and Glorious Martyrdoms of Several Young Persons, who suffered Death with the most cruel Tortures for the Profession of True Religion. To which is Added an Account OF GOD's Gracious Dealings with some Young Persons and Children: and of their ... Holy and Exemplary lives ... with Pictures, Poems, and Spiritual Songs proper to the Subject.*

London. Later editions 1709, 1720.

Preface: 'It is a common saying that Examples prevail more upon Persons than Precepts ... for how many (Young Persons especially) are

in this last and worst Age of the World, Debauched and Ruined by the
Examples of their Companions ... so that there is a great need of using
all Endeavour to prompt Youth to that which is Good, they being
Naturally addicted to be drawn aside by their own corrupt Inclinations.'

Includes: Early Christian martyrs Agnes, Cecilia and Theodora.

1675

14   *Phillips, Edward. *Theatrum Poetarum or a compleat collection of the
poets of all ages ... particularly those of our own nation.*

London. 2 parts. Later enlarged edition 1800.

Phillips was Milton's nephew and biographer; his Appendix includes
'Women among the moderns eminent for poetry', listing Anne
Broadstreet, Astrea [sic] Behn, 'Dramatic writer, so much the more
considerable as being a Woman, to the present English Stage',
Catherine Philips, 'the most applauded, at this time, Poetess of our
Nation', Margaret, Duchess of Newcastle, Mary Morpeth, 'a Scotch
Poetess' and Lady Mary Wroth.

1678

15   Crouch, Nathaniel (pseud: Robert Burton). *Remarks upon the lives of
several Excellent Young Persons of both sexes ... who have been
Famous for Vertue and Piety*

Printed by Tho. James for Nath. Crouch, London. Later editions
1695, 1713, 1725.

Pirated from Janeway and expanded.

Crouch was a popularizing publisher of shilling books for young
autodidacts.

Includes: Martyrs Agnes, Eugenia, Theodora, Cecilia and Julietta
with pictures of their executions as well as Lady Jane Grey and 'the
Troubles of Queen Elizabeth in her youth before she came to the
Crown'. Strongly Protestant, with sensational illustrations for the
young mind to dwell on.

1682

16   Crouch, Nathaniel (pseud. Robert Burton). *Admirable Curiosities
Rarities and Wonders in England, Scotland and Ireland. An Account of
many Remarkable Persons, and Places etc.*

Printed by Tho. Snowden for Nath. Crouch at the Bell, next to
Kemp's Coffee House, Exchange Alley over against the Exchange in
Cornhill, London.

Reprinted or new editions 1684, 1685, 1710, 1718, 1737, 1811.

Sensational anecdotes, county by county, for example, Queen Emma's Tryal by Ordeal 1053 and Lady Godiva in Coventry, both illustrated. Also Isabel of Arundel 1250, Protestant women martyrs, and Mary, Queen of Scots.

4. Mrs Katherine Clark, from Samuel Clark, *The Lives of Sundry Eminent Persons in this Later Age,* Part Two, 1683.

1683

17   Clark, Samuel. *The Lives of Sundry Eminent Persons in this Later Age. Part 2, Of Nobility and Gentry of both sexes.*

Thos. Simmons, London. Folio.

A much more temperate and humane work than his earlier volume of 1646 – chastened by defeat? Puritan testimony to outstanding Englishwomen on the godly side in the Civil War and/or Restoration.

Preface by Richard Baxter: 'God will have the memory of the just to be blessed, and the names of the wicked to rot. ... And the true History of exemplary lives is a pleasant and profitable recreation to young persons. ... O how much better work it is than cards, Dice, Revels, Stage-Plays, Romances or idle chat.' The author 'was not to patch or paint the dead ... but to deliver the naked Truth'. Clark includes: Mrs Mary Gunter, Lady Alice Lucy, Lady Mary Vere, Mary, Countess of Warwick, Lady Mary Armine, Lady Elizabeth Langham, Susannah, Countess of Suffolk, Katharine Brettarg, Margaret Baxter and his own wife. 'Nobility is not hereditary but inherent'; therefore these women were memorable for their steadfastness and compassionate generosity to victims of the Civil War and for their private virtues of Humility, Patience, Self-examination and Zeal. His own wife Katherine 'was often a Spur but never a Bridle to him in those things which were good ... She never grutched nor grumbled ... and [in dying after 50 years of marriage and nine children] did wear out, not rust out: Burn out, was not blown out.'

Note that Anne, Countess of Coventry's *Catalogue of Books* (1704), includes this work, and that John Wesley used extracts from it for *A Christian Library*.

1684

18   P.W. *The History of Witches and Wizards Giving a true Account of all their Tryals in England, Scotland, Sweedland, France and New England, with their Confessions and Condemnation*. London.

Promises much more substance than it can produce; in fact it is a small chapbook with crude woodcuts and consists of sensational anecdotes, including a fragment of the Faust tale and Hodge the conjuror as well as references to Sir Matthew Hale. Asserts that belief in Satan is evidence of the reader's nonatheism. Includes Juliana Cox of Taunton, executed 1663 for being unable to recite correctly 'lead us not into temptation', Elizabeth Styles of Blyford, Anne Bishop, Alice Duke, Agnes Sympson and Ann Duny among other persecuted old women.

1685

19   Sinclar, George. *Satan's Invisible World Discovered – A Choice Collection of Modern Relations, proving evidently against the Saducees and Atheists of this present Age, that there are Devils, Spirits, Witches and Apparitions, from Authentick Records; Attestations of Famous Witnesses and undoubted Verity.*

John Reid, Edinburgh. Later editions 1769, 1808, 1871.

The late Professor of Philosophy from Glasgow fights a last, terrible stand against the coming Enlightenment, opposing Hobbes, Spinoza and Descartes as well as Quakerism: 'that sink of folly and madness'. He recounts with incredible credulity and misogyny the trial of the Paisley 'witches', including 80-year-old Margaret Jackson, Jennet Mathie, Bessie Weir and Marjorie Craig as well as the old widow Elizabeth Graham, who died 'obdurate'.

1686

20   *Shirley, John. *The Illustrious History of Women or a compendium of the many virtues that adorn the fair sex.*

J. Harris, London.

Exemplary listing based mostly on classical literary anecdote, under headings including Piety, Liberality, Learning and Painting. Shirley champions women's intellectual equality:

> It is plain, Man having attain'd the upperhand in Rule and power ... strives to keep that state as his prerogative, by endeavouring to keep the softer sex in Ignorance; and to Effect this, he uses his utmost endeavours to possess her with a belief of her Incapacitie. ... There is an equality of the soul; ... women's wisdom is nothing inferior, nor their Thoughts confin'd to narrower limits than what comprehend the souls of men.

1688

21   Crouch, Nathaniel. *Female Excellency or the Ladies' glory Illustrated in the worthy Lives and memorable Actions of Famous Women, who have been renowned either for Virtue or Valour in several Ages of the World.*

3rd edition by N. Boddington and J. Blare, London. Later enlarged editions 1696, 1699, 1728.

Pocketsize book for a lady's bookshelf. British Library copy has name of 'Susanna Miller' on flyleaf.

Includes: Deborah, Judith, Esther, Susanna, Lucretia, Boadicea, Mariamne, wife of Herod, Clotilda of France, Andegora of Spain as well as Mary Tudor and Elizabeth I.

1693

22   Tate, Nahum. *A Present for the Ladies, being an Historical Account of Several Illustrious Persons of the Female Sex.*

Printed for Francis Saunders, at the Blue Anchor in the New Exchange in the Strand. London. 2nd edition.

Author always in debt and seeking literary patrons. This 'Present' is dedicated to the Countess of Radnor: 'There is not one Virtuous or Commendable Qualification, but what have been possest by the Fair Sex, and that in the most transcendent Degree.' Quaint, flowery, discursive, sincere (?) knight-errantry, championing the nobility of women.

Includes anecdotal references to Adesia, Aspasia, Diotima, Cornelia,

Zenobia, Portia, Paulina, as well as 'the daughters of our own Sir Anthony Cook' and Elizabeth I. Peroration:

> The Inference to be naturally drawn from [these] Illustrious Instances is That we should at last render to this NOBLE SEX their just Respect and Honour. That we should no longer look upon them as the Entertainments of idle Hours, but place them in that venerable Esteem that is due to their Merit.

1695

23 Du Fresnoy, C. A. *The Art of Painting with Remarks translated into English by Mr Dryden, as also a Short Account of the most Eminent Painters, both Ancient and Modern.*

Printed by J. Heptinstall for W. Rogers at the Sun against St Dunstan's Church in Fleet St.

No women among the ancient masters, but the modern masters include Marietta Tintoretta and Artemisia Gentileschi.

1697

24 Evelyn, John. *Numismata – A Discourse of Medals.*

B. Tooke, London.

Lists those 'Learned, Virtuous and Fair' illustrious women whom Evelyn would have liked to have seen commemorated on a medal. Includes: 'Boadicea, Cordelia, Queen Emma, Elfreda, Abbess Hilda, Julian Barnes [Berners], the lady Jane Grey, Elizabeth Carew, Lady Mary Nevil, Mrs Roper, Mrs Weston, Ann Ascue [sic], Catherine Kiligrew and her sister, Mary Countess of Pembroke, Lady Arabella Stuart, Anne Cooke, Elizabeth I, the Duchess of Newcastle, our Sappho Mrs Behn, Mrs Makins, Madam Astall of the most Sublime: Besides, what lately she has proposed to the Virtuous of her Sex, to shew by her own Example, what Great Things, and Excellencies it is Capable of, and which call to mind the lady of the Protestant Monastery, Mrs Farrer, not long since at Geding in Huntingdonshire.'

1703

25 *Tomkins, John, Field, J., Bell, J., Wagstaffe, T., Kendall, John, and others. *Piety Promoted in Brief Memorials of the Virtuous Lives, Services and DYING SAYINGS of some of the People called Quakers.*

London. 1703–1774.

Expanded editions in 1711, 1721, 1759–1771. Later editions 1789, 1811, 1823, 1854.

Cumulative communal project. It is noteworthy that the 1811 edition copy in the BL has the autograph of Elizabeth Fry. Originally intended for 'the young of both sexes'. Many Quaker women's intrepid travels, defiance of the state and public testimony to their beliefs despite persecution are recorded:

'Great was their faith, zeal and labour ... for they could not but speak the things which they had seen and heard ... 'Manifold were their sufferings ... as whipping and beating till their flesh was like a jelly, knocking down, and sore abuses in public places of worship, and in markets and streets; ... besides long imprisonments under praemunire, and otherwise, in nasty jails and dungeons, and holes, whereby many lost their lives.'

Includes: Anne Camm, Elizabeth Braithwaite, Lucy Chopping, Priscilla Cotton, Mary Dyer, Margaret Fell, Mary Mollineux, Elizabeth Rathbone, Joan Vokins and Anne Whitehead i.a. An important source for women's history.

1708

26 Downes, John. *Roscius Anglicanus*, or *An Historical Review of the Stage After it had been suppressed by means of the late Unhappy Civil War begun in 1641 till the time of King Charles II's Restoration in May 1660. Giving an Account of its Rise again; of the Time and Places the Governours of both the companies first Erected their Theatres, the Names of the Principal Actors and Actresses who Perform'd in the Chiefest Plays; and Modern Poets for the space of 46 Years, and during the Reign of Three Kings, and part of our present Sovereign Lady Queen ANNE. From 1660–1706.*

Printed and sold by H. Playford, at his House in Arundel St near the Water-side, London. Later editions 1789, 1792, 1886.

Facsimile edition by Montague Summers. Fortune Press, London. 1928.

Not always accurate but still a unique, idiosyncratic account of Restoration stage-history including original cast-lists of first English actresses. Includes Mrs Ellin Gwyn (i.e. Nell Gwynn), Mrs Ann Marshall, Mrs Rutter, Mrs Corey, Mrs Boutel, Mrs Davenport, (later Mrs Betterton,) Mrs Davids, Mrs Saunderson, Mrs Ann Gibbs, Mrs Barry, Mrs Bracegirdle and Mrs Oldfield. Indispensable explanatory notes in the 1928 edition by Montague Summers.

5. The actress Mrs
Bracegirdle, from
*Women of History by
Eminent Writers,*
1874.

1719

27   Jacob, Giles. *The Poetical Register.*

E. Curll, London. 1719–20.

a) *The Lives and Characters of the English Dramatists, with an Acct. of
their Writing.*

Acknowledges help of Langbain, Prior and Congreve. Richard
Savage also supposed to have been a contributor. Admiring of Aphra
Behn: 'She had a strong Natural Genius.' Lists seventeen plays by her
with their stage-history. Also includes Frances Boothby, Susanna
Centilevre, Mrs Davis, de la Riviere Manley ('deservedly esteem'd for
her Affability, Wit and Loyalty . . . in all [her writings] there appears a
happy Sprightlinesse and an easy Turn') Katharine Philips, who
equalled the Lesbian Sappho according to Langbain; Mary Pix,
Catherine Trotter, later Cockburn, and Mrs Wiseman.

b) *An Historical Acct. of the Lives and writings of our most
considerable English poets.*

Includes: Centilevre, Chudleigh, Mrs Martha Fowke, Mrs Molesworth (i.e. Mary Monck), Anne, Countess of Winchilsea, and
Elizabeth Rowe.

1721

28 Strype, John. *Ecclesiastical Memorials relating chiefly to Religion and the reformation of it and the emergencies of the Church of England under King Henry VIII, King Edward VI and Queen Mary.*

Printed for John Wyat at the Rose, St Paul's Churchyard, London. Folio. 3 volumes. Last edition 1822.

The second volume by Strype, an important compilation of essential documents of the mid-sixteenth century includes the invocation of the Arian, Joan Bocher, of her friend Anne Askew before she in turn is burned at the stake. Strype's other volumes include Anne Boleyn's last letters to Henry VIII, and documents relating to Catherine Parr, Mary Tudor and Elizabeth I.

1722

29 *Sewel, William. *History of the Quakers.*

J. Sowle, London. Folio.

Recommended by Charles Lamb 'above all church-narratives'; a vivid, detailed history of the persecution and steadfastness of Quakers, including many women, 1646–1717. Testifies to the amazing travels, hostility and hardships endured by the earliest Quaker women preachers. Includes: Anne Audland, Barbara Blaugdone, Antonia Bourignon, Anne Burden, Sarah Cheevers, Mary Clark, Anne Coleman, Anna Curtis, Ann Downer, Mary Dyer, Princess Elizabeth of the Palatinate, Catherine Evans, Margaret Fell, Mary Fisher, Elizabeth Fletcher, Sarah Gibbons, Sarah Goldsmith, Elizabeth Heavens, Elizabeth Hooton, Mary Sanders, Sarah Sawyer, Anna Maria van Schurman, Hannah Stranger, Hannah Wright and Judith Zinspenning – the author's Dutch mother. An important, underused source.

1733

30 *Besse, Joseph. *An Abstract of the Sufferings of the People called Quakers . . . from 1650, to . . . 1689.* Taken from original records and other authentick accounts.

Luke Hinde, London. 1733–8. 2 volumes. New edition 1753.

Graphic, county by county record of the persecution of individual women, for example:

> 1656, Isabel Barlow for speaking to the People in Ampthill Market was committed to Bridewell, order'd to be whipt and kept there about a month. . . . 1658, Mary Akehurst of Lewes, going into the Steeplehouse

... and asking a Question of an Independent Priest who had then preached, was hal'd out by the People and afterward by her Husband so beat and pinch't, that she could not lift up her Arms to her Head without pain.

Besse includes Mary Fisher, preacher to Cambridge students and to the Sultan of Constantinople. See also *Testimonies of Deceased Ministers*, or 'Public Friends', from 1760 on. All such Quaker collective biography would have had an exclusively Quaker readership; its influence, via women readers, on all eighteenth- and nineteenth-century emancipatory movements, including the emancipation of women, has still not been adequately acknowledged. A rich, underused source.

1738

31   Tootell, Hugh. *The Church History of England 1500–1688 chiefly with regard to Catholicks, being a complete account of the ... various fortunes of the Catholick cause ... particularly the lives of the most eminent Catholicks ... who have distinguished themselves by their piety, learning or military abilities.*

Published in Brussels under the pseudonym 'Charles Dodd'.

Republished London 1839–43.

Volume 2 includes 'Lives of women under Elizabeth': Jane Berkely, Margaret Clement, Margaret Clitheroe, Margaret Ward, Anne Line, Isabel Sackville the last Abbess and Mary Stuart. Notable for praising that intrepid pioneer of girls' education, Mary Ward, 'a gentlewoman of singular zeal and qualifications', though it does not treat the whole of her life.

1740

32   Wilford, John. *Memorials and Characters together with the Lives of divers eminent and worthy persons ... the most celebrated examples of piety and virtue among the Nobility, Gentry and Clergy, from 1600– present.*

J. Wilford, London. 1740–1.

A compilation of funeral orations, monotonous spiritual panegyrics on many strict Anglican ladies including Anne Baynard, Catherine Bovey, Elizabeth Burnet, Lady Cutts, Lady Gethin, Susanna Hopton. A source for Ballard (see entry 38) and Gibbons (see entry 55).

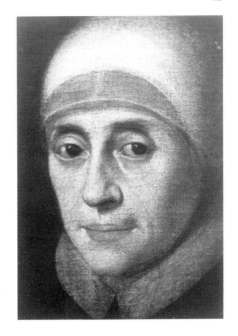

6. Mary Ward, educationalist, foundress of the Institute of the Blessed Virgin Mary. Original in the Institute of the Maria Ward Schwestern, Augsburg.

1741

33 Betterton, Thos. *History of the English Stage from the Restauration to the present time. Including the lives, characters and amours, of the most eminent actors and actresses. Complied by Edmund Curll and William Oldys from the notes of Betterton.*

E. Curll. London.

Gossipy anecdotes about actresses including Nell Gwyn, Mrs Barry, Mrs Bracegirdle and a long memoir of Mrs Oldfield.

34 Challoner, Richard. *Memoirs of Missionary Priests and ... of other Catholics of both sexes, that have suffered death in England on religious accounts, 1577–1684.*

Published anonymously, London. 2 parts. Later editions 1803, 1836, 1842, 1878, 1924.

Challoner was Bishop of Debra.

The Catholics' answer to Foxe's *Book of Martyrs*, 200 years on. Challoner's aim was to make English Catholics aware of their continuity with the Old Church and with the martyr/saints of their own country. Note his phrase 'Prisoner for ... conscience'. Includes: Margaret Clitheroe, Margaret Ward, Ann Line, all executed under Elizabeth I.

7. The actress Mrs
Oldfield, from E. Robins,
*The Palmy Days of Nance
Oldfield*, 1898.

1745

35   Challoner, Richard. *Britannia Sancta* or *The lives of the most
celebrated British, English, Scottish and Irish Saints who have
flourished in these Islands, from the earliest times of Christianity,
down to the change of religion in the 16thC.*

First published anonymously by Thomas Meigham, London. 2 parts.

Self-explanatory.

1747

36   Oldys, William. *Biographia Britannica* or *The lives of the most eminent
persons who have flourished in Great Britain and Ireland, from the
earliest ages, down to the present times – Statesmen, Prelates, Patriots,
Lawyers, Divines and whoever else have been eminent for Wisdom,
Learning, Valour or other laudable accomplishments … digested in the
manner of Mr Bayle's historical and critical dictionary.*

W. Innys, etc., London. 1747–66. 6 volumes.

The earlier English version of Bayle, translated with commentary and
additions by Barnard, Birch and Lockman, 1734, had added Anna
Comnena, Arabella Stuart, Aphra Behn, Boadicea, Anne Boleyn,
Louise Labé, Katherine Philips, Elizabeth Rowe, Anna Maria
Schurman, Anne Wharton and Anne, Countess of Winchilsea to

the pantheon. Oldys includes very few women: Arlotta, mother of William the Conqueror, Aphra Behn, Arabella Stuart, Lady Jane Grey, the Duchess of Newcastle and Elizabeth Rowe. Mrs Oldfield is just a footnote to the life of Farquahar, Mary Astell a footnote to the Revd Smallridge. The *Supplement* includes Catherine Cockburn as 'a remarkable instance of extraordinary genius for literature in the female sex' and Anne Manley, author of *New Atlantis*.

37   Anon. *The Female Rebels.*

Edinburgh.

Misogynistic: 'This Part of the Species are the first proselytes to the most absurd Doctrines and in all Changes of State or Religion, the ladies are sure to lead the Van.' Accuses 'the titular Dutchess of Perth' and Lady Ogilvie of sadistic cruelty both to British prisoners and to common soldiers in the Jacobite army. Respectful to Flora MacDonald.

1752

38   *Ballard, George. *Memoirs of Several Ladies of Great Britain who have been celebrated for their writing or skill in the learned languages, arts and sciences.*

Printed for the Author, Oxford. (By subscription).

Dedicated to Mrs Delany, artist and correspondent of Swift, Richardson, Handel and Reynolds.

Influenced by Foxe and inspired by the neglected Anglo-Saxon scholar Elizabeth Elstob who had compiled and handed over to Ballard a list of 40 names (now lost). Ballard selected 64 (generally upper-class and Anglican) ladies self-taught in Classics and/or theology. Ballard included Margery Kempe, Julian of Norwich, Juliana Berners, Margaret Roper, Catherine of Aragon, Anne Askew, Catherine Parr, Lady Jane Grey, Lady Elizabeth Fane, Mary, Countess of Arundel, Lady Mary Howard, Mary Tudor, Lady Anne, Lady Margaret and Lady Jane Seymour, Elizabeth Dancy, Mary Roper, Margaret Clement, Cecilia Heron, Margaret Ascham, Mary, Queen of Scots, Lady Burleigh, Lady Bacon, Lady Russel, Katherine Killigrew, Elizabeth I, Elizabeth Weston, Lady Arabella Seymour, Mary, Countess of Pembroke, Lady Elizabeth Davies, Katherine Chidley, Katherine Philips, Margaret, Duchess of New-castle, Anne Killigrew, Anne Baynard, Lady Gethin, Lady Halket, Susanna Hopton, Elizabeth Burnet, Lady Chudleigh, Lady Masham, the Hon. Mrs Monk, Lady Pakington, Anne, Countess of Winchil-sea, Catherine Bovey, Constantia Grierson and Mary Astell. He called Astell's *Serious Proposal for ... a female college* 'a noble design', deploring its frustration by Bishop Burnet. Ballard's

8. The poets Katherine Philips and Anne Killigrew, from *Women of History by Eminent Writers*, 1874.

subscription list is especially interesting for its evidence of a network of supporters of women's educational potential – both men and women. (Richardson and the youthful Gibbon were among the subscribers). Ridiculed by Oxford's gentleman scholars of the day, Ballard's innovative and scholarly enterprise was immediately saluted as inspirational for girl readers: 'To younger minds it must inspire a desire of learning.' Ballard's *Memoirs* are now acknowledged to be 'a landmark in the history of feminism' (Ruth Perry, Introduction to her edition of Ballard, 1985). Ballard's Anglican bias led him to overlook the Catholic educationalist Mary Ward, the Catholic convert Lady Falkland, Quaker religious writers such as Margaret Fell and, of course, the Restoration wits Aphra Behn, de la Riviere Manley and Susannah Centilevre. (See Margaret Ezell, *Writing Women's Literary History* (1993)). The pressure on Ballard, however, to demonstrate that women's learning did not have to mean irreligion or immorality is clear from Mrs Chapone's letter to Richardson, 24 November 1750. (See Forster Collection of Richardson's Correspondence, FM XII, 2, ff.16–18, Victoria and Albert Museum).

1753

39　　*Cibber, Thos. *et al. Lives of the Poets of Great Britain and Ireland, to the time of Dean Swift. Compiled from materials scattered in a variety of books.*

R. Griffiths, London. 5 volumes.

Really written by Robert Shiels, Johnson's amanuensis. Includes Susanna Centilevre, Catherine Cockburn, Laetitia Pilkington, Mary Chandler, Mrs Manley, Elizabeth Rowe and Elizabeth Thomas. Defends Behn, Centilevre and even Pilkington against 'supercilious prudes', being sympathetic to those who must 'write or starve'. 'Anecdotal, readable, irresponsible' according to Donald Stauffer, *The Art of Biography in 18th Century England* (NY, 1941).

40   Burnham, Richard. *Pious Memorials or the Power of RELIGION upon the mind in Sickness and at Death: Exemplified in the Experience of many Divines and other Eminent Persons ... Interspersed with what was most Remarkable in their lives. From Bede to the present.*

J. Oliver, London.

Late Puritan work hoping to animate the unbeliever, the libertine, the gay and indolent to die rejoicing in the faith. Overwhelmingly male but includes Mrs Baily, Mary Corbet, Mary Dolittle, Margaret Ducke, Mrs Houfmans, Queen Joan of Navarre and Elizabeth Wilkinson.

1754

41   *Duncombe, John. *The Feminiad: a poem.*

London.

Not itself a collective biography but rather a celebratory listing in verse of 'female genius' for later biographers to work on. Adds Frances Brooke, Elizabeth Carter, Hester Chapone, Mary Leapor, the working-class woman poet, but not Mary Collier the washer-woman poet, to the roll-call. He is the first to mention the Wesleys' doomed sister, Hetty, the poet Mehetabel Wright. Duncombe very probably introduced Hetty Wright's poems, including those on *Clarissa*, to Richardson, whose novel may have been in part inspired by her tragic life story. For Duncombe, see Jocelyn Harris, Introduction to *The Feminiad* (Augustan Reprint Society, 1981).

1756

42   Butler, Alban. *Lives of the Fathers, Martyrs and other Principal Saints compiled from Original Monuments and other Authentic Records.*

First published anonymously in London. 1756–9. 12 volumes.

Later editions in 1779, 1799, 1812, 1833, 1836, 1847, 1850, 1857–60, 1883–6, 1926–38, 1949.

The classic Calendar of Saints. Predominantly male but includes tributes to the holy self-abnegation and self-mortification of Saints

Agnes, Agatha, Genevieve, Clare, Colette, Scholastica, Maud, Withburge, Anastasia, Clotilda, Etheldreda, Bridget, Rose, Catherine, Theresa and Apollonia. Original Preface describes Saints as 'the greatest [personages] who have ever adorned the world ... our future companions in eternal glory [teaching us] humility, meekness and ... patience.' The archbishops and bishops affixed their approbation to the Dublin edition of 1779, expressing their 'ardent desire, that a copy of it were placed in the hands of every family of the ... people committed to our care'.

1758

43   Walpole, Horace. *A Catalogue of the Royal and Noble Authors of England, Scotland, and Ireland.*

Strawberry Hill. 2 volumes.

Later editions 1759, 1796, London, Dublin, Edinburgh.

Adds Frances Thynne, Duchess of Somerset, and Anne Howard, Viscountess Irwin, in lively, literary survey including much quotation.

See also the same author's *Anecdotes of Painting with some account of the principal artists, 1762–1771.* Strawberry Hill, London. 2 volumes. He pays tribute to Mrs Delany in later editions.

1760

44   Ffloyd, T. *Bibliotheca Biographica: A Synopsis of Universal Biography, Ancient and Modern, containing a circumstantial and curious Detail of the Lives, Actions and Opinions, Writings, and characters of the most celebrated Persons, of both Sexes, of all Ranks, in all Countries, and in all Ages.*

London. 3 volumes.

A haphazard, cosmopolitan collection; includes 'learned ladies' as well as actresses, adventuresses and every queen. Ample, even prolix and sympathetic entries on Mary Astell, Elizabeth Barton, Aphra Behn, Mrs Betterton, Mrs Bracegirdle, Susanna Centilevre, Lady Chudleigh, Catherine Cockburn, Constantia Grierson, Anne Killigrew, Mrs Manley ('much superior to what is usually found among her sex'), Mrs Masham, Anne Oldfield, Katherine Philips, Elizabeth Rowe and Elizabeth Thomas. A helpful, underused source.

1762

45 Chambers, E. *et al. A New and General Biographical Dictionary Containing An Historical and Critical Account of Eminent Persons in every Nation particularly the British and Irish From the Earliest Accounts of Time to the present period.*

London. 12 volumes.

Based on Bayle and British predecessors. Overwhelmingly male but does include St Catherine, Catherine de Medici, Mary Chandler, Mary Chudleigh, Cleopatra, Catherine Cockburn, Anna Comnena, Anne Dacier, Mary Eagle, Elizabeth I, Lady Grace Gethin, the Gonzaga sisters, Mary de Jars Gournay, Lady Jane Grey, Mme de Guyon, Heloisa, Hypatia, Anne Killigrew, Mme de Maintenon, Margaret Duchess of Newcastle, Mary Tudor, Mary, Queen of Scots, Mary Monk, Olympia Morata, Anne Oldfield, Catherine Phillips, Laetitia Pilkington, Elizabeth Rowe, Anna Maria Schurman and Lady Winchilsea. Its 1767 supplement added Joan of Arc, Mary Astell, Mrs Charke the autobiographer, Mrs Cibber, 'regarded as the greatest actress in England', Lady Elizabeth Hastings, Catherine Parr and 'Corinna' Thomas.

1764

46 Baker, D. E. *The Companion to the Play-house: or, an Historical account of all the dramatic writers – and their works – that have appeared in Great Britain and Ireland, from the commencement of our theatrical exhibitions, down to 1764.*

London.

Volume 1 is a dictionary of published plays.

Volume 2 is a biographical dictionary 'of every Dramatic Writer and of our most celebrated actors who were also authors of theatrical compositions'.

Sympathetic to Aphra Behn who was 'oblig'd to comply with the corrupt taste of the times.' Quotes her woman friend's memoir testifying to her personal qualities. Calls Mrs Centilevre 'the first of our female wits – she has but one above her – the great Mrs Behn'. Long entry on Charlotte Charke, who joined 'the most wretched of all human beings, the members of a meer strolling company of Actors.' Also mentions Kitty Clive, Eliza Heywood, Anne, Countess of Winchilsea, Frances Sheridan and Catherine Trotter, later Cockburn.

Useful.

1766

47   Anon. *Biographium Femineum* or *The Female Worthies ... or Memoirs of the most illustrious ladies of all ages and nations who have been eminently distinguished for their magnanimity, learning, genius, virtue, piety, and other excellent endowments.*

S. Crowder, London. 2 volumes.

Preface: 'The education of women has, in general, been too much confined, and their employments, chiefly, of a domestic nature; and in these modern times of luxury and dissipation, parents seem to be of the opinion, that if they can but teach their children to dance, dress according to the mode, ogle and catch admirers, their fortune is made. ... But how unlike the studies and applications of the *British* ladies ... about a century or two ago! ... Souls are of no sex, any more than wit, genius, or any other of the intellectual faculties.' [Ends with passage from More:] 'May you meet with a wife who is not always stupidly silent, nor always prattling nonsense.'

An ambitious, literary, predominantly English coverage. But the range does include Acme, a Jewess, Arete, a teacher of philosophy, Antoinette Bourignon, a famous French enthusiast, Joan of Arc, Charixena, a learned Grecian lady, Queen Christina of Sweden, Helena Lucretia Cornaro, made a doctor at Padua, Cassandra Fedele, a Venetian lady, the Gonzaga sisters, Heloisa, Hypatia, Mary de Jars Gournay, Madame de Maintenon, Olympia Morata, Sappho and Mme de Sévigné. Refuses to include courtesans and deliberately omits details of Centilevre's private life. The English pantheon includes Anne Askew, Mary Astell, Aphra Behn, Anne Broadstreet, Katherine Chidleigh 'a violent independent', Catherine Cockburn, Julian of Norwich, Margery Kempe, Damaris Masham, Anne Oldfield, Laetitia Pilkington, Lady Elizabeth Hastings, Elizabeth Rowe, and 'Dean Swift's wife Stella' to the listing of Elizabethan aristocratic women scholars.

Could the anonymous compiler of this work have been a woman?

1769

48   Granger, James. *A Biographical History of England from Egbert the Great to the Great Revolution ... adapted to a methodical catalogue of engraved British heads, etc.*

London. 1769–74. 3 volumes. Later enlarged editions 1775, 1779, 1804, 1824.

Annotated history of extant portraits. Includes Susanna Perwich, musician and composer. Most of the (few) other women entries are royalty, aristocracy or the king's mistresses, thus qualifying by birth or beauty alone.

1772

49   Towers, Joseph, D. D. *British Biography* or *An accurate and impartial account of the lives of Eminent Persons, Wicliff to the present: Statesmen, Philosophers, Patriots, Poets, Generals, Lawyers, Admirals or Divines.*

London. 10 volumes. Folio.

Given this definition of 'eminence' most women find no way of entry; the few women who are included are usually footnotes and/or victims, for example, Elizabeth Barton, the 'Holy Maid of Kent' is a footnote to the life of Bishop Fisher, Alice Perrers is a footnote to the life of William of Wykelm, Joan Bocher, 'Anabaptist', a footnote to Cranmer, and the Baptist martyr, Mrs Elizabeth Gaunt, burnt for sheltering a runaway after Sedgemoor, 1685, the last woman executed on political grounds in Britain (and first mentioned in Burnet's *History of His Own Times* and Crosby's *History of the English Baptists*, 1711) is here a footnote to Judge Jeffreys. The ideological perspective is of anti-Papist Enlightenment disgust at 'bigotry, religious persecution, injustice and cruelty'. Queens, of course, are included and some women writers – Behn, Cockburn and Rowe. Swift's Stella is a five-page footnote to Swift.

Note Towers' *Dialogues Concerning the Ladies to which is added An Essay on the Antient Amazons*, T. Cadell, London, 1785, no. 2 'On examples of women's knowledge of classics', and no. 7 'On ladies who have distinguished themselves by their literary talents': 'At no preceding period has there ever been in England ... so many female authors as at present, and possessed of such indisputable merit.'

50   Anon. *Theatrical Biography, or Memoirs of the principal performers of the three Theatres Royal.*

S. Bladon, London. 2 volumes.

Self-explanatory.

1774

51   *Scott, Mary. *The Female Advocate. A poem occasioned by reading Mr Duncombe's Feminiad.*

Published by radical bookseller Joseph Johnson, London.

First biographical listing by a named woman author, though not itself a work of collective biography. See Gae Holladay, Introduction to *The Female Advocate* (Augustan Reprint Society, William Andrews Clark Memorial Library, University of California, LA, 1984).

Fervently feminist introduction by Scott: 'All I contend for is, that it is a duty absolutely incumbent on every woman whom nature hath

9. The 'Blue-stockings', Mrs Montagu and Elizabeth Carter from Clarke, *The Georgian Era*, vol. 3, 1834.

blest with talents ... to improve them; and that that is much oftener the case than it is usually supposed to be.' Like Duncombe, a versified listing of those women who deserve to be remembered. To Duncombe, Scott both adds a reminder of all the brilliant Renaissance women scholars in England and brings the story up to date with appreciative praise of the 'Blue-stockings', Mrs Barbauld, Mrs Chapone, Sarah Fielding, Mrs Macaulay, Mrs Montagu and Hannah More. Mary Scott is also the first to include the freed slave poet Phillis Wheatley as writing poems of 'considerable merit'. Huntingdon Library copy, 1774, inscribed 'Sarah Froud'.

1776

52   Noorthouk, J. *Historical and Classical Dictionary containing the lives and characters of the most eminent and learned persons of every age and nation, from the earliest period to the present time.*

London. 2 volumes.

Short entries on Behn, Centilevre, Chudleigh, Cockburn, Grierson, Manley, Philips, Rowe and Anne, Countess of Winchilsea, as well as on queens.

53   Hawkins, Sir John. *A General History of the Science and Practice of Music.*

T. Payne, Mews-Gate, London. 5 volumes.

Dedicated to George III.

Volume 3 includes Elizabeth I, Volume 4 Mrs Bracegirdle, Mary Davies, Mrs Cross and Mrs Cibber and Volume 5 includes Mrs Tofts, Signora Margarita, Anastasia Robinson, Francesca Cuzzoni and Elisabeth La Guerre, all practising musicians, mostly singers.

54   Burney, Dr Charles. *A General History of Music from the Earliest Ages to the Present Period.*

With plates, including a portrait. Printed for the Author, London. 1776–89.

4 volumes. Later editions 1782–89. Last edition 1935.

Later volumes mention many women singers and performers, among them Agujari, Anna de Amicis, Mrs Arne, Bertolli, Mrs Betterton, Mrs Billington, Mrs Bracegirdle, Mrs Campion, Mrs Cibber, Kitty Clive, Cuzzoni, Cecilia Davies, Faustina, Colomba Mattei, Anastasia Robinson and Mrs Tofts i.a.

1777

55   Gibbons, Thos. D. D. *Memoirs of eminently pious women who were ornaments to their sex, blessings to their families, and edifying examples to the Church and World.*

J. Backland, London. 2 volumes. Later enlarged editions 1804, 1815, 1838.

Prefaced by long address 'to Parents on the education of their Children and particularly their Daughters.' Reads like a throwback to the Puritanism of the seventeenth century but is in fact also a bridge leading to the Evangelicalism of the early nineteenth century. Based on Clarke, Wilford and Ballard, with references to Foxe; panegyrics to Margaret Andrews, Katharine Brettarg, Lady Catherine Courtney, Lady Margaret Houghton and Mrs Jane Ratcliffe, in addition to the now traditional Protestant heroines Anne Askew, Lady Jane Grey, Catherine Parr and Lady Rachel Russell.

1778

56   Kippis, Andrew, D. D. with Towers, Joseph, D. D. *Biographia Britannica.*

C. Bathurst, London. 1778–93. Vols 1–5. Folio.

Adds Mary Astell, quoting her feminist views but judging her 'much over-rated by Ballard and others'. Includes Behn, having not read her on principle: 'to her indelible disgrace her talents were prostituted to licentious purposes'. Admits 'the considerable powers of imagination and invention' of the Duchess of Newcastle, despite her 'absurd ... pretensions'; respects Catherine Cockburn and grants short entries to Charlotte Charke, Mrs Delany and Elizabeth Elstob. Otherwise overwhelmingly masculine with almost a whole volume given to Captain Cook. Reaches only F in the alphabet.

1780

57 *Thicknesse, Ann. *Sketches of the Lives and Writings of the Ladies of France*.

London. 1780–2. 3 volumes. (Published by subscription).

The first specialized work of collective biography by a named woman author.

Introduction: 'If women are thought to possess minds less capable of solid reflection than men they owe this conjecture entirely to their own vanity and erroneous mode of education. ... That Nature is not in fault, we can prove, by setting forth so many examples of women who have made a considerable figure in the republic of letters. ... England has thitherto produced but very few; among the most distinguished of whom we are happy to name a Carter, an Aikin [i.e. Mrs Barbauld], a

10. Ann Thicknesse, née Ford, by Gainsborough, 1760; and Ninon l'Enclos, from the frontispiece to Thicknesse's *Sketches of the Lives and Writings of the Ladies of France*, 1780.

Chapone and a Montagu. [But] in France not less than four hundred women have been renowned for their literary talents.' Survey ranges from Heloise to Louise Labé, Mlle de Gournay, Mme de Scudery, Mme de Sévigné, Ninon l'Enclos, Mme de Maintenon, Mme de Lambert, Mme Dacier, Mme Guyon and Mme de Riccoboni, i.a. Note Donald Stauffer's belittling comment on Thicknesse: 'A Church-of-England, prudent, sentimental housewife tries to support herself by re-telling to her subscribers anecdotes of all sorts.' (*The Art of Biography in 18th C. England, Bibliog. supplement*, NY (1936), p. 246).

1782

58   Reed, Isaac. *Biographia Dramatica* or *A Companion to the Playhouse.*

London. 2 volumes.

Continuation of D. E. Baker 1764 (entry 46) taking stage-history to 1782.

59   Nichols, John. *Biographical and Literary Anecdotes of William Bowyer, Printer, F.S.A. and of many of his learned friends containing an incidental view of the progress and advancement of literature in this kingdom 1700–1777.*

Printed by and for the author, London.

Indexed, but not easy to navigate dense footnoting of interesting publishing information on, among others, Mary Astell, Elizabeth Blackwell, Frances Brooke, Catherine Cockburn, Elizabeth Elstob, Eleanor James, Frances Sheridan, Lady Sundon (née Clayton), Catherine Talbot and Anna Williams, scientific friend and blind protégée of Dr Johnson.

1790

60   Pulteney, Richard. *Historical and Biographical Sketches of the Progress of Botany in England from its origin to the introduction of the Linnaean System.*

T. Cadell, London. 2 volumes.

Exclusively male with the important exception of Elizabeth Blackwell for whom 'physic is indebted for the most complete set of figures of the medicinal plants.'

61   Anon. *The Beauties of Biography for the Young of both Sexes*

An abstract of earlier biographical compendia. Only three women: Behn, Centilevre and Elizabeth Thomas in Volume 1 and Laetitia Pilkington and Elizabeth Rowe in volume 2.

11. Reynolds' portraits of Mrs Abington in Congreve's *Love for Love*, 1771, and of Mrs Siddons as The Tragic Muse, 1789.

62   Haslewood, Joseph. *The Secret History of the Green Rooms – authentic and entertaining memoirs of the Actors and Actresses of the three Theatres Royal: Drury Lane, Covent Garden and the Haymarket.*

London. 3 volumes. New editions 1792, 1793, 1975.

Pirated from *Theatrical Biography*, 1772 (see entry 50) with updating.

Includes short notes on 30 actresses both famous and forgotten.

1791

63   *Benger, Elizabeth. *The Female Geniad – a poem ... written at the age of 13.*

T. Hookham and J. J. Carpenter; C. and G. Kearsley, London.

Artless, ardent championing of the intellectual powers of women by a child of 13.

Preface: 'Zeal for the honour of my sex, and admiration of shining merit, prompted [me] to celebrate the female writers ... may their bright examples animate the rising fair of Britain!' Her versified listing begins 'Hail Female Geniuses! ... /A boundless theme, yet bards neglect to sing' and happily moves from Sappho to Caroline Herschel, Angelica Kauffmann and Fanny Burney.

Elizabeth Benger grew up to write a biography of Anne Boleyn.

1794

64   Milner, Joseph. *The History of the Church of Christ. Vol. 1 The first Three Centuries.*

J. Matthews, York and London.

An account by an Augustinian Calvinist of the persecution of the Early Christians, including the martyrs Blandina, Potamiaena, Marcella, Donata, Vestina, Felicitas and Perpetua, all tortured to death in the amphitheatres of the Roman Empire.

1795

65   Seward, William. *Anecdotes of some distinguished persons chiefly of the present and two preceding centuries.*

Cadell and Davies, London. 4 volumes.

Writer a learned friend of Dr Johnson. He cites original documents. Except for Joan of Arc, the women here, unlike the men he discusses, are all distinguished by the accident of royal or noble birth rather than by their personal gifts or achievements. Includes Catherine of Aragon, Blanche Arundell, Anne Boleyn, Lady Jane Grey, Mary Tudor, Mary, Queen of Scots, Elizabeth I, Lady Arabella Stuart, Anne, Countess of Dorset, Henrietta Maria, Catherine de Medici, Queen Anne, Queen Caroline, Queen Christina of Sweden, the Duchess of Marlborough, Lady Fanshawe and Mme de Sévigné.

1798

66   Polwhele, R. *The Unsex'd Females.*

Cadell and Davies, London.

Anti-Jacobin, misogynist versified listing of reprehensible radical women headed by Mary Wollstonecraft, followed by Mrs Barbauld, 'Perdita' Robinson, Charlotte Smith, Mrs Yearsley, Mary Hays and Angelica Kauffmann. Deeply unpleasant triumphing that M. W. 'died a death that strongly marked the distinction of the sexes' in footnote omitted in 1810 edition. Polwhele much prefers Mrs Montagu, Mrs Carter, Mrs Chapone, Anna Seward, Mrs Piozzi, Fanny Burney, Mrs Radcliffe and, above all, Hannah More. Women divided according to their political position vis-à-vis the French Revolution.

67   Rawes, W. *Examples for Youth: remarkable instances of Early Piety.*

London.

Selected from J. Tomkins' *et al. Piety Promoted.* (See entry 25).

Note Mary Ann Kelty's later *Memoirs and Persecutions of Primitive Quakers* (1844).

68   *Pilkington, Mary. *A Mirror for the Female Sex – Historical Beauties for Young Ladies intended to lead the Female Mind to the Love and Practice of Moral Goodness. Designed principally for the use of Ladies' Schools.*

London. Later editions 1799, 1800.

Preface: 'The fruit of extensive reading, this work was suggested by Dodd's *Beauties of History* written for the edification of his own sex. Teaching of history should not be confined to recounting the competitions of nations ... the horrors of battles, the havock of sieges, the achievements of heroism, and the bickerings of faction.' Moralistic anecdotes exemplifying 'Religion', 'Filial duties', 'Fortitude', etc. Protestant heroism.

1799

68a   Aikin, Dr J. *General Biography* or *Lives Critical and Historical of the most eminent persons of all ages, countries, conditions and professions.*

G. G. and J. Robinson, London. 1799–1818. 10 volumes.

Overwhelmingly male; a few intellectually distinguished women, in addition to the crowned female heads, especially Christina of Sweden, but no new entries.

68b   *Robinson, Mary (using pseudonym of Randall, Anne Frances). *A Letter to the Women of England on the Injustice of Mental Subordination. With Anecdotes.*

'Wherefore are we
Born with high Souls, but *to assert ourselves?*'
                                                    Rowe

Longman and Rees, London. No. 39.

The author, a former actress, royal mistress, novelist and poet known as 'Perdita', wrote this attack on marital despotism using collective biography to affirm the intellectual and moral capacity of women – as illustrated from ancient times up till Marie-Antoinette and

12. Lady Mary Wortley Montagu
from *Women of History by
Eminent Writers*, 1874.

Charlotte Corday. Ends with a list of British female literary figures
living in the eighteenth century, including: Barbauld, Carter,
D'Arblay, Hays, Inchbald, Macaulay, Montagu, More, Piozzi,
Thicknesse, Wollstonecraft, Williams and Yearsley, i.a. among
others.

1800

69 Watkins, John. *An Universal Biographical and Historical Dictionary
containing a Faithful Account of the Lives, Actions and Characters of
the Most Eminent Persons of all Ages and all countries.*

R. Phillips, London.

Overwhelmingly male but includes very short entries on Mary Astell,
Mary Beale, Aphra Behn, Susanna Cibber, Mary Delany, Mary
Wortley Montagu, Anne Oldfield, and Peg Woffington among
others.

1801

70 Cumming, Susannah. *Juvenile Biography* or *Lives of Celebrated
Children inculcating virtue by eminent examples from real life, to which
are added moral reflections addressed to the youth of both sexes.*

London.

Translation of book by French Royalist émigré, M. Josse.

Despite unpromising title and intrusively moralistic commentary,
some stirring tales for girls, for example:

Hal-mehi Cantimiri of Kurdistan – True courage is the offspring of the soul. ... A girl at 12 years old has more aptitude, sense and penetration and ... is more useful in her father's house than a dozen boys of the same age. It is, perhaps, on account of these excellent qualities that ungrateful, jealous and despotic men constantly keep women from solid studies, under the absurd pretext that the affairs of house-keeping must be their principal occupation.

Mothers are warned against pushing their daughters into being mere precocious little performers of dance or music instead of acquiring a serious education that might enable them to survive, if reduced to penury and exile by a catastrophe such as the French Revolution.

1803

71   Owen, William. *The Cambrian Biography* or *Historical Notices of Celebrated Men among the Ancient Britons.*

E. Williams, London.

Some women listed as daughters or mothers of eminent Welshmen.

72   *Anon. *Eccentric Biography* or *Memoirs of Remarkable Female Characters Ancient and Modern including Actresses, Adventurers, Authoresses, Fortune-Tellers, Gipsies, Dwarfs, Swindlers, Vagrants*

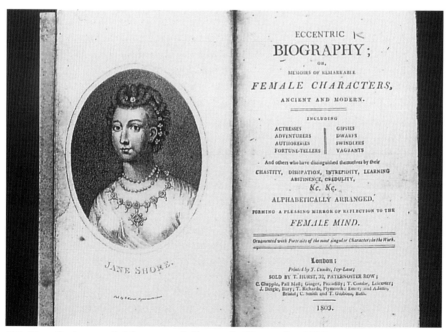

13. Frontispiece and title-page of *Eccentric Biography*, 1803.

*And others who have distinguished themselves by their Chastitie,
Dissipation, Intrepiditie, Learning, Abstinence, Credulity etc. forming
a pleasing mirror of reflection to the FEMALE MIND.*

Printed by J. Cundee, Ivy-Lane, 1803, London. Illustrated.

Preface: 'Conscious that a work of this kind must be eagerly perused
by ladies in particular ... every due attention has been paid to the
style and language, and tho' some of our pages may be filled with the
memoirs of celebrated Courtezans, not a sentence, not a word has
been admitted that can give the least offence to the most reserved
delicacy.' Includes Mary Astell, Elizabeth Barton, Aphra Behn, Mrs
Bellamy, Mrs Centilevre, Charlotte Charke, Susannah Cibber, Kitty
Clive, Catherine Cockburn, Charlotte Corday, Mary Fisher, Mary
Frith, Mrs Montagu, Mme Roland, 'perhaps the most extraordinary
woman that this or any other age has produced.' Sympathetic to the
point of sentimentality re Mary Wollstonecraft.

73   *Hays, Mary. *FEMALE BIOGRAPHY* or *Memoirs of illustrious and
celebrated WOMEN of all ages and countries.*

R. Phillips, London. 6 volumes.

The first heterogeneous collective biography of women in English by
a named woman author.

Preface: 'My pen has been taken up in the cause, and for the benefit,
of my own sex. ... Women, unsophisticated by the pedantry of the
schools, read not for dry information, to load their memories with
uninteresting facts. ... Their understandings are principally acces-
sible through their affections: they delight in minute delineations of
character; ... I have at heart the happiness of my sex, and their
advancement in the grand scale of rational and social existence. ...
To excite a worthier emulation, the following memorial of those
women, whose endowments, or whose conduct, have reflected lustre
upon the sex, is presented more especially to the rising generation.'

Given Hays' focus on the 'Illustrious' in her title, there is a
preponderance of crowned heads. Not only Elizabeth I but also
Mary, Queen of Scots, Christina of Sweden and above all Catherine
II of Russia have almost book-length entries.

Hays includes: Joan of Arc, Anne Askew, Mary Astell, Mary Beale,
Aphra Behn, Anne Bradstreet, Elizabeth Elstob, Anne, Countess of
Winchilsea, Sarah Fielding, Mary Fisher, Anne Killigrew, Mary
Leapor, Mrs Oldfield, Susanna Perwich, Laetitia Pilkington, and
Lady Rachel Russell, i.a. What is new is Hays' politically radical
inclusion of a lengthy condensation of the Girondin Mme Roland's
Memoirs and even a short entry on Charlotte Corday – 'she mistook
her victim. It was Robespierre that marked with indelible stain the

cause of liberty.' Hays' comments and selected quotations are frequently feminist, notably re Centilevre, Cibber, Chapone, Chudleigh and Cockburn. Among her surprising omissions are Mary Collier, Margaret Fell, Elizabeth Gaunt, Elizabeth Carter and other Blue-stockings, Mary Wortley Montagu, Mrs Delany and, above all, her friend Mary Wollstonecraft Godwin – perhaps an entry made impossible in her view by Godwin's all-too candid revelations.

It may be relevant that Mary Wollstonecraft herself, in her most egalitarian Revolutionary period, could see no role for the collective biography of women in the struggle for women's liberation into the ranks of rational citizens. The extraordinary are no help to the ordinary, the 'Great' to the obscure:

> I shall not lay any stress on the example of a few women who, from having received a masculine education, have acquired courage and resolution. [Footnote]: Sappho, Eloisa, Mrs Macaulay, the Empress of Russia, Mme d'Eon etc. These, and many more may be reckoned exceptions; and, are not all heroes as well as heroines, exceptional to general rules? I wish to see women neither heroines nor brutes, but reasonable creatures.
>
> (*Vindication of the Rights of Women*, 1792)

The most original entry in Hays is on the politically radical historian, Catharine Macaulay, based on contemporary oral sources and depicting a girl who, having one found her way into her father's library 'rioted in intellectual luxury'. Jane Austen's sister-in-law owned a copy of this work.

73a   Kirby, R. S. *The Wonderful and Scientific Museum: or Magazine of Remarkable Characters.*

R. S. Kirby, London. 1803–1820. Illustrated. 6 volumes.

More or less innocent sensationalism in a totally haphazard sequence of anecdotes, unified only by their being 'extraordinary'. Among dogs, volcanoes, dwarfs, bearded women and the original Robinson Crusoe are found the beggar Ann Siggs, the perjurer Elizabeth Canning, the gypsy Mrs Squire and, in later volumes Mother Shipton, the exchange broker Theodora Grahn, the soldiers Mary Talbot, Hannah Snell, Christian Davies and Renée Bordereau as well as alleged witches, Joan of Arc, the prophetess Johanna Southcott and the convicted criminal Mary Bateman. Kirby was particularly intrigued by women who passed as men. Interesting to see what the uneducated book-buying public found riveting.

14. The soldier Hannah Snell and the prophetess Johanna Southcott from Kirby's
Wonderful and Scientific Museum or Magazine of Remarkable Characters, 1803–20.

1804

74   *Pilkington, Mary. *Memoirs of Celebrated Female Characters who
have distinguished themselves by their talents and virtues in every age
and nation containing the most extensive collection of illustrious
examples of Feminine Excellence ever published.*

London. Illustrated.

Cheap pocketbook edition of 346 pages from actress Mrs Abington
to Zosima, intended both for young readers and the general public.

Preface: The author has always endeavoured 'to lean to the
favourable side in judging a character'. On the bland side, therefore,
managing to be both full of praise for Mme Roland and very
sympathetic to Marie-Antoinette. In favour of Mary Astell, ascribes
Aphra Behn's freedoms and levities to her times and very
sympathetic to Mary Wollstonecraft Godwin who 'possessed that
vigour of understanding, which even those who were prejudiced
against her could not but admire.' Admires 'her strong, disinterested
power of attachment' but deplores her deviation from 'the path of
purity'. Very good illustrations of Inchbald, Siddons, Hannah More,
Mrs Trimmer and Charlotte Smith.

75   *Betham, Matilda. *A Biographical Dictionary of the Celebrated
Women of Every Age and Country.*

B. Crossby and Co., London. c. 850 pp.

Many more women intellectuals, poets and, above all, artists included by Betham, herself a miniaturist painter, and friend of the Lambs, than by Hays or Pilkington. Much less Eurocentric than Hays; Peruvian, Tartar, San Domingan, Hindu, Moghul, Jewish, Moorish and Japanese women are also mentioned, if briefly. Includes Sophonisba Angusciola, Joan of Arc, Anne Askew, Aspasia, Mary Astell, Mary Beale, Aphra Behn (respectful and exonerating), Antoinette Bourignon, Frances Brooke, Camma, Rosalba Carriera, Susanna Centilevre, Catherine Cockburn, Helena Cornaro, Mrs Delany (full of praise), Elizabeth Elstob, Cassandra Fidelis, Sarah Fielding, Mary Fisher, Artemisia Gentileschi, Lady Mary Wortley Montagu, Mary Wollstonecraft Godwin ('this singular woman') Marie de Gournay, Heloise, Hildegarde of Bingen, Hypatia, Julian of Norwich, Mary Leapor, Ninon l'Enclos, Anne, Countess of Winchilsea, Catharine Macaulay ('the democratic spirit of her writings has made them fall into dispute'), de la Riviere Manley, Damaris Masham, Noor Jehan, Maria Sybilla Merian, Anne Oldfield, Laetitia Pilkington, Mme Roland, Elizabeth Rowe (long entry), Anna Maria Schurman, Mme de Sévigné, Frances Sheridan ('Her *Sidney Biddulph* may be ranked with the first productions of that class in our or any other language'), Teresa of Avila, Marietta

15. Frontispiece to Betham's *Biographical Dictionary of the Celebrated Women of Every Age and Country,* 1804.

Tintoretta, and Peg Woffington. Betham is critical of women in power who abused that power inhumanely, e.g. Isabella of Castile and Catherine de Medici.

Her sources extended to include Thicknesse and *Le Dictionnaire des Femmes Célébres* for French women and Italian women, Bruce's *Travels* for African women, Josephus' *History of the Jews*, *Bibliothecae Arabico-Hispanae Escurialiensis* for Moorish women, Joseph Milner's *History of the Church of Christ* for earliest Christians, and Dow's *History of Hindostan*, as well as the *Abecedario Pittorico* for women painters.

For Matilda Betham herself see Matilda Betham-Edwards, *Six Life-Studies of Famous Women*, 1880 (entry 205).

1806

76 Stewarton. *The Female Revolutionary Plutarch, Containing Biographical, Historical, and Revolutionary Sketches, Characters and Anecdotes.*

John Murray, London. 3 volumes.

Dedicated to Marie-Antoinette: 'Her murder is still unrevenged!!!' Tendentious, scandalous – not to say libellous – gossip of the time, targeting revolutionary women. Attacks Mme Roland, Mme de Stael, and Theroigne de Mericourt, 'the Jacobin Harlot'.

77 Brydges, Sir Samuel Egerton. *Censura Literaria – Titles, Abstracts and Opinions of Old English Books with General Disquisitions, articles of Biography and other Literary Antiquities.*

Longman, Hurst, Rees, London. 1805–9. 10 volumes.

Eccentric but fascinating antiquarian jottings with some rare biographical material on, among others, Elizabeth Carew, Sarah Scott, Mrs Montagu, Elizabeth Carter, Mehetabel Wesley Wright, Charlotte Smith, Hester Chapone, Ann Lefroy, Elizabeth, Lady Cary, and 'Perdita' Robinson.

78 Wilson, W. *The Eccentric Mirror reflecting a faithful and interesting delineation of male and female characters particularly distinguished by extraordinary qualifications, talents and propensities, natural or acquired.*

London. 1806–13. 4 volumes. Illustrated.

Strange mixture of entries includes male impersonators such as Mary Anne Talbot, Chevalier D'Eon, and Mary East, Nell Gwynne, a centenarian Philadelphia slave 'Alice', and the Blue-stockings, Mrs Montagu and Mrs Delany.

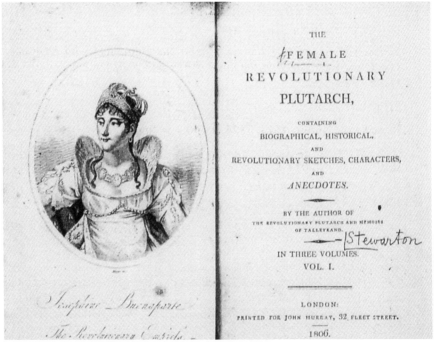

16. Frontispiece and title-page of Stewarton's *The Female Revolutionary Plutarch*, 1805.

1808

79   Gilliland, T. *The Dramatic Mirror: containing the History of the Stage, from the earliest period to the present time; including A biographical and critical account of all the Dramatic Writers, from 1660; and also of the most distinguished performers from the days of Shakespeare to 1807.*

Printed for C. Chapple, Pall Mall, London. Several volumes.

Short entries. Includes singers such as Angelica Catalina.

80   Bogue, D. and Bennett, J. *History of Dissenters 1688–1808.*

Printed for the authors, London. 1808–12. 4 volumes.

Volume I's respectful Quaker section mentions Mary Fisher and Ann Austin, Volume II mentions Lady Lisle, Elizabeth Gaunt, and Queen Mary, Volume III includes Lady Huntingdon and Volume IV Cromwell's granddaughter, Mrs Bendish and Mrs Elizabeth Rowe.

1809

81 Knapp, A. and Baldwin, W. *The Newgate Calendar, comprising interesting memoirs of the most notorious characters who have been convicted of outrages on the laws of England since the commencement of the 18th Century.*

Printed for Nuttall, Fisher and Dixon, Liverpool.

Reprinted London 1819, 1826, 1828. 4 volumes.

Updating of R. Sanders' *Newgate Calendar*, 6 volumes, 1764, and of William Jackson's *New and Complete Newgate Calendar*, or *Villany displayed in all its branches*, 6 volumes, 1796–1800.

Grim reading. The lawyer authors Knapp and Baldwin are compassionate towards prostitutes and seduced girls who commit infanticide. Includes the notorious Elizabeth Brownrigg, as well as women executed for killing violent husbands.

82 Aikin, Dr J. Continuation of his *General Biography* or *Lives Critical and Historical of the most eminent persons of all ages, countries, conditions and professions.*

G. G. and J. Robinson, London. 1799–1818. 10 volumes. See entry 68a.

83 Kirby, R.S. Continuation of his *The Wonderful and Scientific Museum: or the Magazine of Remarkable Characters.*

R. S. Kirby, London. 1803–1820. Illustrated. 6 volumes. See entry 73a.

1810

84 *Aikin, Lucy. *Epistles on Women exemplifying their character and condition in various ages and nations.*

J. Johnson and Co., London.

Lucy Aikin was the historian niece of Mrs Barbauld and the daughter of Dr J. Aikin and friend of Elizabeth Benger.

Introduction:

> Let me ... disclaim ... the absurd idea that the two sexes ever can be, or ever ought to be, placed in all respects on a footing of equality. ... As long as the bodily constitution of the species shall remain the same, man must in general assume those public and active offices of life which confer authority. ... No! instead of aspiring to be inferior men, let us content ourselves with becoming noble women ... but let not sex be carried into everything. Let the impartial voice of History testify for us, that, when

permitted, we have been the worthy associates of the best efforts of the best of men; ... [There] is not an endowment or propensity, or mental quality of any kind, which may not be derived from her father to the daughter, to the son from his mother.

Therefore Lucy Aikin hopes

'for a future when scholars, sages, patriots will treat women as sister and friend. The politic father will not then leave as a "legacy" to his daughters the injunction to conceal their wit, their learning, and even their good sense, in deference to the "natural malignity" with which most men regard every woman of a sound understanding and cultivated mind. ... It is impossible for man to degrade his companion without degrading himself, or to elevate her without receiving a proportional accession of dignity and happiness. Milton was blasphemous in making his Eve say to his Adam "God is thy head, thou mine".'

Lucy Aikin's verse is even more radical, rebelliously contemptuous towards subservient women 'taught with spaniel soul to kiss the rod/ And worship man as delegate of God.' Ends 'O Woman, rise! be free!'

85   Barbauld, Anna Laetitia, completed by Aikin, Lucy. *The British Novelists including [short] biographical and critical introductions to each author.*

F. C. and J. Rivington, London. 1810–24. 48 volumes.

Includes: Charlotte Smith, Mrs Inchbald and Frances Brooke, i.a.

1810

86   Gould, John. *Dictionary of Painters, Sculptors, Architects and Engravers: Biographical Sketches of Eminent Artists.*

London. Later edition 1834.

Enlargement of Walpole's *Anecdotes of Painting*, 1762–71 (see entry 43). Includes Lucia and Sophonisba Angusciola, Artemisia Gentileschi, Mary Beale, Maria Sibylla Merian, Diana Glauber, Margaret Godewyck and Susan Rose but no Mrs Delany, Maria Cosway or Angelica Kauffmann. And no index, alas.

1812

87   *Chalmers, Alexander. *General Biographical Dictionary – Containing an Historical and Critical Account of the Lives and Writings of the Most Eminent Persons in every nation, particularly the British and Irish, from the earliest accounts to the present time. A new edition, revised and enlarged.*

J. Nichols and Son etc., London. 1812–17. 32 volumes.

Huge, magisterial achievement, summing up the culturally liberal, if politically and morally conservative, judgement concerning which dead deserve to be remembered. Secular, with emphasis on learning, literature and the arts. Very useful as an indicator of which women it was possible for educated Protestant Englishwomen to claim as 'foremothers' in Jane Austen's time. Well indexed and each entry scrupulously referenced. An important source.

Overwhelmingly male but includes: Maria Agnesi, Sophonisba Angusciola, Anna Comnena, Anyta, Arabella Stuart, Tullia D'Aragon, Anne Askew, Mary Astell, Magdalene D'Aubespere, Countess D'Aunoy, Anne Bacon, Mary Anne Barbier, Elizabeth Barton, Laura Bassi, Anne Baynard, Mary Beale, Margaret Beaufort, Aphra Behn – 'her works now deservedly forgotten ... [she] upon the whole cannot be considered as an ornament either to her sex, or her nation' – Catherine Bernard, Juliana Berners, Elizabeth Blackwell, Elizabeth Bland, Boadicea, Mary-Anne Boccage, St Bridget, Frances Brooke, Elspeth Buchan, Elizabeth Carter (long entry), Catherine of Aragon, Catherine Howard, Catharine Parr, Catherine Alexieva, Catherine II of Russia, St Catherine of Siena, Margaret Cavendish, Duchess of Newcastle (long entry), Susanna Centilevre, Mary Chandler, Charlotte Charke, Marchais Castelet, Elizabeth Cheron, Queen Christian, Lady Mary Chudleigh, Cleopatra, Anne Clifford, Kitty Clive, Catherine Cockburn (long entry), Henrietta Coligini, Mildred, Elizabeth and Katherine Cooke, Piscopia Cornaro, Sophia de Cottin, Hannah Cowley, Elizabeth Creed, Maria Cunitz, Mrs Delany (long entry), Joan Durmee, Elizabeth I of England, Elizabeth of Austria, Elizabeth of Russia, Elizabeth Elstob, Erinna, Eudocia, Artemisia Gentileschi, Lady Grace Gethin, Mary Wollstonecraft Godwin, 'who unfolded many a wild theory on the duties and character of her sex', Lucretia Gonzaga, Mary de Jars Gournay, Lady Jane Grey, Elizabeth Griffith, Mme de Guyon, Lady Anne Halket, Lady Elizabeth Hastings, Mary Jeanne L'Heritier, Eliza Heywood, Antionette des Houlieres, Mary Huber, Hypatia, Mary Catherine des Jardins, Pope Joan, Joan of Arc, Angelica Kauffman, Louise Labé, Marchioness de Lambert, Mary Leapor, Charlotte Lennox (long entry), Margaret de Lusson, Catherine Macaulay (condescending and critical of her politics), Mme de Maintenon, Mary I of England, Mary, Queen of Scots, Mary II of England, de la Riviere Manley, 'compares unfavourably with the superior accomplishments of her sex in our days ... very low in the scale of female authors', Lady Damaris Masham, Mary Monk, Lady Mary Wortley Montagu, Elizabeth Montagu, Olympia Morata, Ann Oldfield, Catherine Philips, Laetitia Pilkington, Christine de Pisan, Anastasia Robinson, 'Perdita' Robinson, Anne Rohan, Mme Roland, Elizabeth Rowe, Sappho,

Anna Maria Schurman, Mme de Scudéry, Mme de Sévigné, Anne Seward, Mary Sidney, Mme de Staal (not Stael), Sulpicia, Catherine Talbot, Elizabeth Thomas, Elizabeth Tollet, Sarah Trimmer, Elizabeth Jane Weston, Anna Williams and Zenobia.

All in all, contains impressive ammunition against the restrictive stereotyping of women.

1813

88 Caulfield, James. *Portraits, Memoirs and Characters of Remarkable Persons from the reign of Edward III to the end of the reign of George III, completing a 12th [i.e. lowest] class of Granger's Biographical History of England.*

R. S. Kirby, London. 1813–19. 3 volumes.

Fascinating and often terrible record of women notorious in folk-memory, including Elizabeth Sawyer, executed 1621 after torture for 'witchcraft', Moll Cut-purse the highwaywoman, Mary Carleton, actress, hanged at Tyburn 1672, Mary Aubrey, burned for killing her violent husband, 1687, Elizabeth Canning wrongly transported for perjury, Christian Davies and Hannah Snell the female soldiers, and Margaret Finch, Queen of the Gypsies. Reveals an underworld of brutalization as well as tough endurance in its sequence of old prints

17. Mary Carleton, actress, conwoman and thief, from Caulfield's *Portraits, Memoirs and Characters of Remarkable Persons*, 1813–19.

showing female centenarians, prostitutes, procuresses, poisoners, female sextons, bone-setters, visionaries who keep company with Jonathan Wild and Dick Turpin.

1814

89   Mills, Dr Alfred. *Biography of Eminent Persons with portraits.*

Minute volume 2″ square, suitable for small infant hands. Queen Eleanor of Acquitane and Lady Jane Grey are the only two women included.

1816

90   Colburn, Henry. *Biographical Dictionary of the Living Authors of Great Britain and Ireland comprising Literary Memoirs and Anecdotes of their Lives.*

London. Dedicated to Prince Regent. 449 two-columned pp.

Overwhelmingly male. Includes Joanna Baillie, Mrs Barbauld, Mary Ann Radcliffe 'one of the Wolstonecraft school', Mary Pilkington, Maria Edgeworth, Lucy Aikin, Matilda Betham, Mary Hays, Helen Maria Williams, Hester Thrale Piozzi (and 'her imprudent marriage').

Some interesting information about very minor writers but no Jane Austen.

1819

91   Ryan, Richard. *Biographies Hibernica – A Biographical Dictionary of the Worthies of Ireland from the earliest periods to the present time.*

R. Ryan, London and Dublin. 2 volumes.

A young man's passionate, patriotic labour of love. Dedicated to the Irish Nation. Preface: 'Biography is of all narratives the most valuable. ... But the deepest and holiest interest is thrown round Biography, when it is appealed to as the vindicator of an unhappy people; when the fallen are forced to bring in the dead to plead their cause. ... The History of Ireland is the most calamitous moral document ... for over six hundred years!'

Mostly male but Volume I includes Mary Barber, Henrietta Lady O'Neil, Charlotte Brooke, Miss Byrne, Susanna Centilevre and Mrs Cleave. Volume II includes Mary Davys, Lady Arabella Denny, Lettice Digby, Catherine Countess of Desmond, Constantia Grierson, Elizabeth Hamilton, Martha Hanna, Alicia Lefanu, Mary Monk, Frances Sheridan, Mary Tighe and Peg Woffington.

1821

92   *Hays, Mary. *Memoirs of Queens illustrious and celebrated.*

T. and J. Allman, Booksellers to her Majesty, London.

Written at the time of the Trial of Queen Caroline (and on her side), the Preface states:

> Having more than once taken up my pen ... in the cause, and for the honour and advantage of my sex, and having deeply at heart ... the moral rights and intellectual advancement of *woman*, I acceded cheerfully, though declining in physical strength and mental activity, to ... compile ... a memoir of *Queens* only, illustrious for their great qualities or celebrated for their endowments and fortunes. I maintain while strength and reason remain to me ... that there can be *but one moral standard of excellence for mankind*, whether male or female, and that the licentious distinctions made by the domineering party, in the spirit of tyranny, selfishness and sensuality, are at the foundation of the heaviest evils that have afflicted, degraded and corrupted society; and I found my arguments upon nature, equity, philosophy and the Christian religion.
>
> The powers and capacity of woman for rational and moral advancement are, at this day, no longer a question: still, her training – tho' superior minds aided by the diffusion of literature, struggle and assert themselves, – is for adornment rather than for use; ... for the delights of the harem, rather than to render her the friend, the companion, the assistant, the counsellor of man.

Eurocentric A–Z of Queens, but also includes Cleopatra, Noor Jehan and Zenobia. Critical of Isabella of Castile and Catherine de Medici.

93   Roberts, Mary. *Select Female Biography: Memoirs of Eminent British Ladies – dedicated to the Ladies of Great Britain.*

J. and A. Arch, London.

Evangelical Preface acknowledges debt to Gibbons' *Pious Women* and to Wilberforce's *Practical Christianity*. Roberts wishes to stress the 'bright examples of suffering virtue, of exalted piety, of active benevolence, and of talents chastened and improved by the noblest principles.' Therefore no actresses or worldly authors. Includes Anne Askew, Lady Jane Grey, Lucy Hutchinson, Lady Rachel Russell, Mrs Elizabeth Rowe, Lady Elizabeth Hastings, Mrs Catherine Hurdis, Catherine Cockburn and Elizabeth Hamilton. Quotes Hannah More on the intellectuals Elizabeth Carter and Elizabeth Smith that 'to know them was to venerate them.' Much emphasis on holy dying.

1823

94   Anon. *Public Characters of All Nations.*

3 volumes.

3000 eminent contemporaries.

Adds Maria Cosway, painter, Hon. Mrs Damer, sculptress, Joanna Baillie, Lucy Aikin and Miss Starke, travel writer.

1824

95   Anon. *The New Female Instructor or the Young Woman's Companion and Guide to Domestic Happiness, being an Epitome of all the Acquirements necessary to form the Female Character in every Class of life with Examples of Illustrious Women.*

London. New edition 1835.

Another Evangelical production. Sandwiched between Medical Receipts, Precepts of Religion and Conduct to Servants are pious entries on Lady Grace Gethin, Katharine Brettarg and Lady Cutts, taken from Gibbons (see entry 55). New entries on Elizabeth Cunningham and the Quaker intellectual, Mrs Knowles, who bested Dr Johnson in argument. Catharine Hurdis, Jane Ratcliffe, Anna Maria Schurman and Elizabeth Smith also included.

96   Sainsbury, John S. *Dictionary of Musicians from the Earliest Ages to the Present – based on Hawkins, Burney, etc.*

Sainsbury and Co., London.

Includes Cecilia Arne, Susannah Cibber, Francesca Cuzzoni, Cecilia Davies, Mrs Lacy, Anastasia Robinson and Mrs Tofts. (See H. G. Farmer in *Music and Letters*, October 1931).

97   Anon. *The Biography of the British Stage – the Correct Narratives of the Lives of all the Principal Actors and Actresses at Drury Lane, Covent Garden, Haymarket, Lyceum, Surrey, Coburg and Adelphi Theatres.*

Sherwood, Jones and Co., London.

Many minor actresses. Their stage-history not their lives are recounted, in contrast to Oxberry (entry 98).

1825

98   Oxberry, William. *Oxberry's Dramatic Biography and Histrionic Anecdotes.*

George Virtue, Ivy-Lane, Paternoster Row, London. 4 volumes.

Edited by a widow who feels free to publish her husband's candid commentary now that he is safely dead. A fascinating, often unflattering compilation of biodata and stage-history, including many Irish and Jewish actresses, their struggles and often bitter marital experience.

Includes: Dorothy Jordan, Frances Kelly, Eliza O'Neill, Mrs Bland, Mrs Mardyn, Mrs Siddons, Elizabeth Billington, Miss Tree and Mrs Harlowe who 'stands forward as the representative of chambermaids, shrews, and old women'. A rich unworked source.

99　　*Taft, Zachariah. *Biographical Sketches of the Lives and Public Ministry of Various Holy Women whose eminent usefulness and successful labours in the Church of Christ have entitled them to be enrolled among the great benefactors of mankind: in which are included several letters from the Rev. J. Wesley never before published.*

'I intreat thee also, true yoke-fellow, help those WOMEN which laboured with me in the gospel, with *Clement* also, and *with* other my *fellow-labourers*, whose names are in the book of life.' Phil. iv, 3. Published for the Author in Leeds and sold in London. 1825–8. 2 volumes. Facsimile reprinted by Methodist Publishing House Peterborough, 1992.

Preface to Volume I: 'Many *females*, whose praise was in all the churches while they lived, have been suffered to drop into oblivion, and their pre-eminent labours, and success in the conversion of souls

18. Mrs Jordan as Hypolita, by Hoppner, from Gerard's *Some Fair Hibernians*, 1897.

to remain as destitute of

to remain as destitute of any public record, as though they had never existed; ... the great majority of Biographers and Editors of Magazines are enemies to female preaching ... except what is found among the *Friends*, or people called Quakers; ... The Rev John Wesley *never* molested any pious female, who was subject to decipline [sic] and order ... but ... gave them encouragement. ... I believe the ordinary call of God to the ministry is to men, and the extraordinary call to females. ... From the pages of History we learn that *women* have ... achieved the most astonishing exploits.' He cites Nehemiah Rogers and Dr Adam Clarke for further, Scriptural authority for the ministry of women. The entire Preface is an important, underused document in the history of the defence of the Christian Ministry of women.

19. (Clockwise) Elizabeth Smith, Ruth Watkins and Mary Barritt Taft, Methodist preachers, c. 1828. Reproduced by courtesy of the Director and University Librarian, the John Rylands University Library of Manchester.

See also Taft's Preface to Volume II justifying his inclusion of female preachers from many different religious communities, not just Methodist, and his *Thoughts on Female Preaching* (1803). The two vols include accounts of Susanna Wesley, Mary Bosanquet, later Fletcher, Elizabeth Tomlinson, later Evans (the aunt of George Eliot and original of Dinah Morris), and 76 other women preachers including thirteen Quakers, among them the anti-slavery missionary in America Catherine Phillips. See Deborah Valenze's *Prophetic Sons and Daughters, Female Preaching and Popular Religion in Industrial England* (1985), for importance of Taft's own wife, Mary Barritt, as a preacher.

1831

100   Jameson, Anna. *Memoirs of Celebrated Female Sovereigns.*

London. 2 volumes. Three later editions, the last in 1869.

Includes: Semiramis, Cleopatra, Zenobia, Joanna I and II, Isabella of Castile, Mary, Queen of Scots, Elizabeth I, Christina of Sweden, Maria Theresa and Catherine II of Russia. Comparative sketches asking what has been the influence of female government on men and nations and what influence the possession of power has had, individually, on the female character? The answer in both cases is sombre – women in power become autocrats.

101   Galt, John. *The Lives of the Players.*

London. 2 volumes. Later edition 1886.

Preface: 'This compilation will probably be among the most amusing books in the language' given its subject. Galt's object is to produce a 'parlour-book', but despite his self-censorship he still has difficulties with the lives of Nell Gwyn, Susanna Centilevre, whose politics were 'zealously attached to Whig principles, more eagerly so, perhaps, than is comely in her sex', Charlotte Charke ('this eccentric damsell'), Mrs George Anne Bellamy, Miss Farren, Sophia Baddeley, Dorothy Jordan, and Mrs Siddons.

1832

102   Tennemann, W. G. *A Manual of the History of Philosophy.*

Oxford. 24 volumes.

Includes Pythagorean women philosophers (not in shortened version of the work).

1834

103 Clarke. *The Georgian Era: The Memoirs of the most Eminent Persons who have flourished in Great Britain till the death of George IV.*

London. 4 volumes.

No women in Volumes I and II except Lady Mary Wortley Montagu. Volume III includes all the 'Blue-stockings' under 'Literature' and adds Hannah Cowley, Felicia Hemans, Sydney Lady Morgan, Caroline Norton, Hester Lynch Piozzi, Amelia Opie, Anna Maria Porter, Jane Taylor, Priscilla Wakefield, and Helen Maria Williams. Positive re Mary Wollstonecraft Godwin:

> *The Rights of Woman* ... a bold and eloquent performance; in which, amid much masculine thought and Amazonian temper, a luxuriance of imagination and trembling delicacy of sentiment ... may be said to have constituted an era in literature, from the extraordinary impression it produced. ... The character of this extraordinary woman ... upon the whole, perhaps, merits our admiration, though not affording a safe model for general imitation.

No Fanny Burney, no Maria Edgeworth and no Jane Austen. Volume IV, under 'Painters' includes only Angelica Kauffmann and, under 'Sculptors', only Anne Damer, compared with nineteen 'Vocal Performers' and 35 women 'Dramatic Performers'.

104 Chambers, Robert (ed.). *A Biographical Dictionary of Eminent Scotsmen.*

W. and R. Chambers, Edinburgh. 4 volumes. 2nd edition 1855, 3rd edition 1870.

Almost no women except Joanna Baillie, Susan Ferrier, Flora Macdonald (under her son), Carolina Nairn and Mary, Queen of Scots. No Covenanting women.

1835

105 Anon. *Biography Illustrated.*

William Darton and Son, London.

Intended for children? BL copy inscribed 'Sarah Basham'. Out of 90 entries on the world's greatest people only ten women: Elizabeth I, Lady Jane Grey, Princess Charlotte, Mme de Genlis, Elizabeth Rowe, Mary II, Elizabeth Viscountess Andover (a 'rare example of virtue in exalted rank'), Queen Charlotte, Lady Rachel Russell and Elizabeth Fry 'whose name has become identified with the cause of humanity', Crabbe's tribute to her.

20. Elizabeth Fry, c. 1834, by George Richmond, in Janet Whitney, *Elizabeth Fry*, 1938.

106   Starling, Elizabeth. *Noble Deeds of Woman or examples of female courage and virtue.*

Henry Bohn, London. 5th edition 1853.

Motto: 'Noble examples excite us to noble deeds' (Seneca).

Very short anecdotes rather than biography, giving real-life examples of filial, sisterly or conjugal heroism, affection, philanthropy, integrity, presence of mind etc. Includes Elizabeth Fry and Grace Darling. Affirms domestic ideology, but insists that 'Woman's sphere of action is not, at all times to be so circumscribed.'

1837

107   Anon. *Memories of Celebrated Women.*

Richard Bentley, New Burlington St, London. 2 volumes.

Advertisement: 'The Work which follows was written some years ago by a lady ... a person of very high talents and information.'

Includes: Joan of Arc, Margaret of Anjou, Lady Jane Grey, Anna Comnena, Mme de Maintenon, Elizabeth I and Maria Pacheo.

21. Frontispiece to
Jameson's *Romance of
Biography*, 1837.

108   Jameson, Anna. *The Romance of Biography or Memoirs of women
loved and celebrated by poets from the days of the troubadours to the
present age; A series of anecdotes intended to illustrate the influence
which female beauty and virtue have exercised over the characters and
writings of men of genius.*

Saunders and Otley, London. 2 volumes.

Extraordinary pot pourri from Ovid to Rousseau and the 'heroines of
modern poetry', and including interesting sidelights on the poets'
lives by foregrounding, for once, the women in those lives. Includes
Petrarch's Laura, Anne Killigrew, Swift's Stella, Pope's Martha
Blount and Lady Mary Wortley Montagu.

109   Jackson, Thos. *A Library of Christian Biography, Vols. 1–12.*

John Mason, London.

Advertisement: 'By describing the origin, the progress, and the results
of personal godliness, it shows us the manner in which we also may
acquire and practise the holiness without which no man shall see the
Lord. ... If others have obtained ... salvation, why should not we?'

Overwhelmingly male but three women entries: Agnes Beaumont,
wrongly accused of poisoning her father, written by herself c. 1700,

Elizabeth Rowe and Lady Elizabeth Hastings, ending with her will, including a charity school for girls, c. 1738.

1838

110 Chambers, R. *Exemplary and Instructive Biography for the Study and Entertainment of Youth.*

W. and R. Chambers, Edinburgh.

All male except for brief notes on Joan of Arc, Elizabeth Benger and Mme de Genlis in miscellaneous notices at the end.

110a Lawrance, Hannah. *Historical Memoirs of the Queens of England from the Commencement of the 12thC.*

Edward Moxon, London.

Preface: 'The queens of England still remain almost unknown. Women, whose importance extended over a wide and important sphere, and whose maternal counsels so frequently impressed a character of good, or ill, on to the reign of the succeeding monarch, have been passed over with scarcely the slightest notice.' Especially interested in the Plantaganet queens' patronage of literature.

See also her later *History of Woman in England and her influence on Society and Literature from the Earliest period, Volume 1 To the Year 1200* (1843). Some primary sources footnoted.

Includes: Queen Maude, Empress Maude, Eleanor of Aquitaine, Isabel of Angoulême, Eleanor of Castile, i.a.

111 Cunningham, G. G. *Lives of Eminent and Illustrious Englishmen from Alfred to the latest times. Illustrated by a series of ... portraits.*

A. Fullarton and Co., Glasgow and Edinburgh. Later editions London, 1840 and 1863–9. 8 volumes.

No women until Volume 8, under 'Literature'. Includes Elizabeth Carter, Anna Seward, Elizabeth Inchbald, Mrs Piozzi, Mrs Radcliffe, Sarah Siddons and Hannah More. No Fanny Burney, Jane Austen, Maria Edgeworth or Mary Wollstonecraft.

1840

111a *Lady Morgan. *Woman and Her Master.*

A. and W. Galignani, Paris.

A cultural survey of women, their civilizing influence and oppressive treatment in tribal societies, Ancient India, China, Egypt, Israel, Classical Greece and Rome. Cites Deborah, Naomi, Ruth, Hannah,

22. Sydney Owenson, Lady Morgan, from Gerard's *Some Fair Hibernians*, 1897.

Abigail, Judith, Esther, Aspasia, Cornelia, Polla Argentaria, Livia, Paulina, Portia, Agrippina, Zenobia, Theodora and Prisca, i.a. The *DNB* dismissive.

112 Strickland, Agnes and Elizabeth. *Lives of the Queens of England, from the Norman Conquest [to the death of Queen Anne]*.

Henry Colburn, London. 1840–48. 12 volumes.

New editions 1851, 1857, 1867, 1878.

Agnes Strickland was the first woman allowed to research in the Public Records Office. See Una Pope-Hennessy, *Agnes Strickland, Biographer of the Queens of England* (1940).

Includes Matilda of Flanders, Matilda of Scotland, Matilda of Boulogne, Eleanor of Provence, Isabella of France, Johanna of Navarre, Margaret of Anjou, Anne Boleyn, Anne of Cleves, Catherine Howard, Catharine Parr, Queen Elizabeth I, Catharine of Braganza, and Mary of Modena by Agnes Strickland; Mary

Tudor, Mary Stuart and Queen Anne and sixteen others by Elizabeth Strickland. The latter was sympathetic to Mary Tudor.

Note the Stricklands' feminine predecessor, Hannah Lawrance's *Historical Memoirs of the Queens of England* (2 volumes, 1838).

1843

113 *Elwood, Mrs A. K. *Memoirs of the Literary Ladies of England from the commencement of the last century.*

London. 2 volumes.

Dedicated to the memory of her mother, Mrs Curteis.

Preface: 'No biography of Literary Females of the past and present centuries [has yet been published]. Intended only for such of her own sex, who, not feeling themselves equal to profound and abstract subjects, can derive amusement and information from what is professedly too light for the learned and too simple for the studious.' Volume I includes all the Blue-stockings, plus Mrs Delany, Lady Mary Wortley Montagu, Charlotte Smith and Fanny Burney. Volume II includes Mrs Piozzi, Jane Austen, Mrs Brunton, L. E. Landon and Mary Wollstonecraft Godwin: '*The Vindication of the Rights of Women* [contains] a bold and original way of thinking; ... she successfully exposes the errors of those theorists who would make woman the mere plaything of man, the eastern sultana ... [But] it is to be lamented that M. W. [intended as] a bright pattern of perfection to her sex, should by her erroneous theories and false principles, have rendered herself instead, rather the beacon by which to warn [women] ... of the rocks upon which enthusiasm and imagination are too apt to wreck their possessor.' Adds tribute to M. W. G. by the late Maria Jewsbury *et al.* and notes that 'the publication of her memoirs by her husband after her death ... [exhibited] errors which love should have concealed.'

An illuminating and overlooked collection of biographical essays.

1845

114 Aguilar, Grace. *The Women of Israel* or *Characters and Sketches from the Holy Scriptures and Jewish History illustrative of the past history, present duties, and future destiny of the Hebrew females, as based on the Word of God.*

London. 600 pp.

6th edition with portrait of author, Groombridge and Sons, London, 1870.

Grace Aguilar was the author of *Words of Israel, Spirit of Judaism* and several novels before her early death. Jewish answer to Christian writers such as Sandford, Ellis and Hamilton who 'believe that Christianity is the sole source of female excellence'. On the contrary, Aguilar asserts, Jewish women had value and dignity long before

23. Frontispiece to Aguilar's
Women of Israel, 1845.

Christianity, which derived its noble estimate of womanhood from
Judaism itself. Includes Eve, Sarah, Rebekah, Leah and Rachel,
Miriam, Deborah, Naomi, Hannah, Michal, Abigail, Esther,
Mariamne and Berenice. Ardent, spiritual, nationalistic Jewish
domestic ideology. Looks forward to the day when girls as well as
boys will have their barmitzvah in the synagogue.

115 Tweedie, W. K. *Select Biographies, ed. for the Wodrow Soc. chiefly
     from mss. in the Library of the Faculty of Advocates.*

     Edinburgh. 1845–7. 2 volumes.

     Includes 'Ladies of the Covenant' – the poet Elizabeth Melville, Lady
     Culross, Lady Binning, Mrs Goodal, Lady Coltness, Lady Anne
     Elcho and Lady Robertland.

1846

116 Anon. *Pen and Ink Sketches of Poets, Preachers and Politicians.*

     Personal memories of Hannah More, Mrs Barbauld, Maria Jews-
     bury, Mrs Hemans, and Joanna Baillie, 'the most powerful of
     England's female writers.'

117 *Costello, Louisa Stuart. *Memoirs of Eminent Englishwoman.*

     Richard Bentley, London. 4 volumes. With portraits.

An important landmark – unVictorian and unjudgemental. Includes: Bess of Hardwick, Arabella Stuart, Catherine Grey, Mary Sidney, Penelope Rich, Magdalen Herbert, Frances Howard, Lady Anne Clifford, Lucy, Countess of Bedford, Queen Elizabeth of Bohemia, Mary Evelyn, Lady Fanshawe, Venetia Stanley, Elizabeth Cromwell, Lucy Hutchinson, Dorothy Sidney, Lady Rachel Russell, Margaret, Duchess of Newcastle, Anne, Countess of Winchilsea, Katherine Philips, Anne Killigrew, Mary Beale, Anne Hyde, Stella and Vanessa, Susanna Centilevre ('this clever and accomplished woman'), the Duchess of Marlborough and Lady Mary Wortley Montagu – the last two being very long essays. Quotes, with disdain, a seventeenth-century 'repressor of liberal education' for women from Lucy Aikin's *James I*. Costello writes from Chatsworth Park.

118   *Balfour, Clara Lucas. *Moral Heroism, or the Trials of the great and good.*

Houlston and Stoneman, London.

Clara Balfour was a pioneer woman, Temperance campaigner and lecturer to the Mechanics' Institute. Caroline Fox's *Journal* gives a vivid and interesting account of her persuasiveness.

Includes chapter on 'Moral heroism exhibited in the female character'. Women are 'the sex called on to endure the greatest amount of suffering. ... No station in life is more important and arduous than that of a wife and a mother. ... The difficulty of pourtraying instances of moral heroism in women, does not arise from scarcity, but is rather the difficulty of wise selection from a mass of material.' Cites women in the Bible from Deborah to Mary Magdalen. Her three more recent instances are Lady Rachel Russell, Isabel Brown the Covenanter's wife, and the late Elizabeth Fry, 'decidedly the most remarkable and admirable woman in this age'.

119   Burns, Revd Jabez. *Mothers of the Wise and Good.*

Houlston and Stoneman, London.

Calvinist reduction of women to their maternal function – anticipates Mrs Ellis, *The Mothers of Great Men* (see entry 144).

1847

120   *Balfour, Clara Lucas. *The Women of Scripture.*

Houlston and Stoneman, London.

Preface: 'The number of admirable books ... during the last twenty years treating of the mental capabilities, moral qualities, and social responsibilities of woman, may seem to render the present work superfluous.' Chapters on Eve, Sarah, Miriam, Deborah, Hannah, Ruth, Naomi and Esther, noting the sufferings of Jewish women from the Ancient Jewish practice of polygamy. Re New Testament women, both in the Gospels and in Paul's Acts and Epistles, Mrs Balfour cites Alley's *Vindicia Christianae*, Chapter 9, concerning the more degrading treatment of women by Ancient Greeks, Hindus and Muslims. Note her Christian maternal feminist peroration: 'Wherever there is ignorance it is [woman's] duty to aim to remove it; wherever there is suffering, it is her privilege to alleviate it; wherever there is impurity, it is her prerogative to destroy it.' Note also Balfour's precursor, Frances King's *Female Scripture Characters* (1813, 10th edition 1826).

121 *Craik, G. L. *The Pursuit of Knowledge under Difficulties. Illustrated by Female Examples. – Being a continuation of The Pursuit of Knowledge under Difficulties, illustrated by anecdotes. (1844)* [i.e. about men].

C. Cox, London.

After general introductory chapters summarizing the controversy over women's intellectual capacity compared with men, two chapters survey women theologians, philosophical writers, mathematicians, astronomers and classical scholars. Individual chapters then given to Elizabeth Smith, Elizabeth Hamilton, Hannah More and Mrs Grant of Laggan. Whereas men have been impeded by poverty, disease and physical handicap, woman's 'sex alone raises a host of difficulties to obstruct her. ... Every woman who has greatly distinguished herself by the cultivation of her intellectual faculties is an example and a marvel.'

It is noteworthy that there is no further edition of this book on women whereas its forerunner, on men, went through several editions, the last in 1906.

1849

122 Smith, William. *Classical Dictionary of Greek and Roman Biography, Mythology and Geography*.

John Murray, London. 3 volumes.

Many later editions, revisions and abridgements.

Includes Aspasia, Corinna, Damophila, Erinna, Phila, Sappho, i.a. from Ancient Greece; and Agrippina, Cleopatra, Clodia, Cornelia, Livia, Julia and Poppaea, i.a. from the history of Ancient Rome.

123 Green, Mary Ann Everett. *Lives of the Princesses of England from the Norman Conquest to 1670*.

24. Madame du Barry, from Kavanagh's *Women in France during the 18th Century*, 1850.

Henry Colburn, London. 1849–55. 6 volumes.

Preface: 'The present field is an untrodden one.' Scholarly, meticulous history of all the royal Englishwomen hitherto overlooked by English historians because they were given in dynastic marriages abroad. Mary Everett Green, née Wood, was the editor of the Calendar of sixteenth- and seventeenth-century English State papers.

1850

124   *Kavanagh, Julia. *Woman in France during the 18th Century*.

London. 2 volumes.

Probing and subtle study of women's influence at court, in the salons and during the Revolution written with political and psychological acumen. Climax is on 'Women in the Reign of Terror'. Though a royalist, Kavanagh has sympathetic respect for defeated Girondins who 'heroically withstood the most fearful tyranny on record'. Re Mme Roland: 'To be faithful to the truth within us is far better, and more noble than to live.'

Note too Kavanagh's predecessor, Mrs Forbes Bush and her *Memoirs of the Queens of France* (1843).

125   Wallace, Robert. *Antitrinitarian Biography or Sketches of the Lives and Writings of Distinguished Antitrinitarians ... from the Reformation to 1700*.

E. V. Whitfield, London. 3 volumes. 1800 pp.

Almost exclusively male except for references to Elizabeth I and to the martyrs Joan Bocher (who is quoted invoking Anne Askew), and 80-year-old Katherine Vogler, burned in Cracow for her Unitarian beliefs. It is interesting to note the list of subscribers to these volumes, including many women, plus Revd William Gaskell.

126 Strickland, Agnes and Elizabeth. *Lives of the Queens of Scotland and English Princesses, connected with the Regal Succession of Great Britain.*

Edinburgh and London. 1850–9. 8 volumes. 2nd edition 1854.

(It was also in 1854 that Mrs Matthew Hall would bring out *The Queens Before the Conquest.*)

1851

127 Anderson, Revd James. *The Ladies of the Covenant. Memoirs of Distinguished Scottish Female Characters embracing the period of the Covenant and the Persecution.*

Blackie & Son, Glasgow. With plates.

More testimony to the continuity of Puritan culture in Britain. Includes Elizabeth Melville, Lady Culross, Mary, Countess of Caithness, Grisell Hume, Lady Baillie, and the martyrs Margaret M'Lauchlan and Margaret Wilson. Preface: 'The Scottish Covenanters were ... no unmeet associates and coadjutators of the prophets and apostles.'

1852

128 *Kavanagh, Julia. *Women of Christianity, exemplary for acts of piety and charity.*

London. With portraits.

Ardent Christian feminist. Preface: 'The good are not alike: they differ from one another as much as other people.' Introduction: 'Christianity and Women':

> Men have filled [History's] pages with their own deeds; ... But in all this what have we? The annals of nations, not the story of humanity. What share have women in the history of men? ... History have been written in the old pagan spirit of recording great events and dazzling actions; ... Christianity proved the charter of [women's] liberty. ... They were now beings with immortal souls; ... They suffered not only for being Christians, but even for exercising Christian virtues: for giving aid and

25. Joan of Arc, from Masson's
*Celebrated Children of All Ages
and Nations,* 1853.

shelter to the living; for burying the dead martyrs. ... Conclusion: When
men liberate nations and win realms, their names live forever. But who
shall count the multitudes these women redeemed from misery?

Includes women martyrs from the Early Church, mediaeval saints,
seventeenth-century French women, ending with Hannah More,
Elizabeth Fry and Sarah Martin.

1853

129 Masson, G. *Celebrated Children of All Ages and Nations.*

George Routledge and Co., Farringdon St, London.

Notable for saccharine version of Joan of Arc pictured not in armour
but in demure, maidenly shift on a hillside.

130 *Hale, Sara Josepha. *Woman's Record, or Sketches of all Distinguished Women from 'the beginning' till A.D. 1850 ... with selections
from female writers of every age.*

New York, English edition, Sampson, Low, Son and Co., London.

The blockbuster – 900 pages and over 2000 entries; a real feat of
digestion, using Biblical, Classical, Italian, French, and German

sources as well as English and American, with an Appendix giving a comprehensive overview of women in the medical missionary field. Acknowledges Mary Hays, Mary Roberts, Anna Jameson, Lady Morgan, Agnes Strickland and Julia Kavanagh among her female predecessors.

> Within the last fifty years more books have been written by women and about women than all that had been issued during the preceding five thousand and eight hundred years. ... The nineteenth century is the Destiny of Woman.

Hale was a forceful Christian feminist, believing passionately in the moral superiority of women: Eve was superior to Adam, Heloise to Abelard, Joan of Arc to all her friends and foes – and Jane Eyre to Rochester. Her woman's eye view of history divides it into four eras: from the Creation until Christ, including his Mother as well as Mary Magdalen; from Christ to 1500, including Hildegarde of Bingen; from 1500 to those dead in 1850, including Anne Askew, Mary Fisher, Elizabeth Blackwell, Mary Leapor, Elizabeth Elstob, Lady Mary Wortley Montagu, Mary Delany, Charlotte Corday, Phillis Wheatley, Jane Austen, Mary Lamb, Elizabeth Fry, L.E.L., Annette von Droste Hülshoff and Grace Aguilar; and, finally, the living. The notable contemporary women whom Hale highlights include Bettina von Arnim, Dr Elizabeth Blackwell, Frederika Bremer, Charlotte Brontë, Elizabeth Barrett Browning, Lydia Maria Child, Angela Burdett Coutts, Dorothea Dix, Aurore Dudevant (i.e. 'George Sand'), Sara Stickney Ellis, Margaret Fuller, Elizabeth Gaskell, Fanny Kemble, Fanny Lewald, Jenny Lind, Harriet Martineau, Mary Russell Mitford, Lucretia Mott, Caroline Norton, Pasta, Rachel, Mary Shelley, Mary Somerville, Harriet Beecher Stowe and Mrs Trollope. All of these are noted for the first time in the history of women's collective biography. Even when she disagrees with more radical feminists such as Mary Wollstonecraft Godwin, Lydia Child (re immediate Abolition), Harriet Martineau or Lucretia Mott, she gives space to their views. Gerda Lerner is mistaken in saying that Hale 'omitted Wollstonecraft ... and included no abolitionists and none connected with the advocacy of woman's rights.' (*The Creation of Feminist Consciousness*, 1993, p. 266). Hale was also the first to include Olympe de Gouges, Lucille Desmoulins and Rachel Varnhagen. A fascinating treasuretrove and landmark in the collective biography of women, it was enthusiastically received and shamelessly plundered for years.

Hale's maternalist feminist credo runs: 'The office of mother is the highest a human being can hold. On its faithful and intelligent performance hangs the hope of the world' [p. 889].

> Wives, mothers, women teachers, women artists, women doctors, and women missionaries are the great civilizers in so far as they help humanity

to become more humane. The reader will easily discover that I place woman's office above man's, because moral influence is superior to mechanical invention, and her peculiar mission is to mould minds, while his deals with material things. [pp. 902–3].

Possibly the strongest statement of Separate Spheres feminism in English. See Ruth Finley, *The Lady of Godey's, Sara Josepha Hale* (1931).

1854

131   Prichard, T. J. L. *The Heroines of Welsh History: comprising memoirs and biographical notices of the Celebrated Women of Wales, Especially the Eminent for Talent, the Exemplary in Conduct, the Eccentric in character and the Curious by Position or otherwise.*

W. F. G. Cash, London.

Some legendary figures include Angharad the Nun, Cordelia, daughter of Lear, Dolly of Pentreath, Elfleda, Ellen Gethin, Nell Gwynn and Princess Nest. See Constance Wall Holt, *Welsh Women* (Scarecrow Press, NJ and London, 1993), for an exemplary modern bibliography on the biography of Welsh women. She recommends T. R. Roberts, *Eminent Welshmen* (1908) and Thos. Rees, *Notable Welshmen* (1908), for their inclusion of Welsh women.

132   *Balfour, Clara Lucas. *Working women of the last half century – the lesson of their lives.*

W. and F. G. Cash, London.

Preface: 'It is hoped the following [pages] . . . will show how much the mind and character of woman have aided the mental and moral progress of the century. The last fifty years have been peculiarly marked by improvement in female education among nearly all classes. This has not been effected *for* woman but *by* her. . . . In order to form correct theories as to what woman might do as a social reformer; it is well to observe what, under great disadvantages, she has done. . . . Woman's mission is best ascertained by a study of those who have fulfilled that mission well.'

Introduction:

[Doing] as well as suffering, thinking as well as feeling, directing as well as obeying, is the providential allotment of woman in our toiling, troubled world. . . . A true appreciation of her responsibilities must lead [woman] to the conviction that she must be the reformer in society. . . . The wrongs of governesses, the wasted health and wretched remuneration of the large class of dressmakers, . . . the long hours of labour in shops, . . . the severe toil of domestic servants; these are social evils immediately appealing to women – in most cases inflicted and perpetuated by them. Then there are far lower depths than these ... the wretched victims of the seducer's art can only be saved ... by woman coming to her rescue. ... The outcast [street]child looks to woman chiefly for the means of escape; for where but to woman should childhood look? The miserable inebriate ... appeals to woman. Biography is peculiarly valuable to woman. She, with her glowing heart and lively fancy, tempted ever into the ideal ... should be a student of the real. Thus the narrative of the joys and sorrows, trials and triumphs, honest mistakes and failures of those [gone before us] ... must be preeminently valuable.

Mentions the inspiration of Elizabeth Fry's example though not included in the book because that life 'is so familiar to all', and then goes on to Mary Carpenter, Caroline Chisholm, Lydia Child and Harriet Beecher Stowe. Lucas also gives chapters to Sarah Trimmer, Hannah More and her sisters, Mrs Barbauld, Elizabeth Smith, Charlotte Elizabeth Tonna, Mrs Sherman, Mary Duncan, Sarah Martin and the early nineteenth-century missionaries and educationalists, Ann Judson and Hannah Kilham.

133   Owen, Mrs Octavius Freire. *The Heroines of History.*

Routledge and Sons, London.

Encompasses the Jewish era with Jael, Judith, Salamona and Mariamne, the Classical era with Semiramis, Penelope, Aspasia, Cornelia, Portia, Cleopatra, Arria, Boadicea and Zenobia and the modern era with Eleanor of Castile, Jane de Montfort, Philippa of Hainault, Joan of Arc, Margaret of Anjou, Isabella of Spain, Catherine de Medici, Lady Jane Grey, Mary, Queen of Scots, Mme de Maintenon and Marie-Antoinette.

134   Toulmin, Camilla. *Memorable Women – The story of their Lives.*

London. 4th edition with illustrations by Birket Foster, London, 1870.

Includes Lady Rachel Russell, Mme D'Arblay and Mrs Piozzi, Mary Ware, Lucy Hutchinson and Lady Fanshawe, Margaret Fuller and Lady Sale, a hostage in the Afghan wars. Illustrates the domestic and private virtues of women: self-denial, fortitude and kindness, thus providing 'an elevating exercise for the opening mind of a youthful female' (*Morning Advertiser*). 'The book is written in a good spirit, and may be placed with safety and profit in the hands of all young women' (*The Athenaeum*). Camilla Toulmin, later Newton Crosland, was a translator of Hugo.

1855

135 Doran, John. *Lives of the Queens of England of the House of Hanover.*

Richard Bentley, London. 2 volumes.

Long studies of Sophia Dorothea, Caroline of Anspach, Charlotte Sophia and Caroline of Brunswick. Mentions Mrs Delany as a harmless old lady, not noticing that she was an artist.

136 Anderson, Revd James. *Ladies of the Reformation – Memoirs of distinguished female characters belonging to the period of the Reformation in the 16thC. ... England, Scotland, and Netherlands.*

Blackie & Son, London. With plates. 715 pp.

Preface: 'The Reformation ... was to the mind of man like a resurrection from the dead. ... A series of biographical memoirs of distinguished females in the principal countries of Europe, who supported or contributed to this great revolution by sympathy, action, or heroic suffering, [has] ... not hitherto been written.' Though holding different Protestant views, they were all united in opposition to the 'Anti-Christ' of Popery. Includes Anne of Bohemia, Queen of Richard II, Anne Boleyn, Anne Askew, Katharine Parr, Lady Jane Grey, Katherine Willoughby, Duchess of Suffolk, Anne de Tserclas, wife of Bishop Hooper, Katherine Vermilia, wife of Peter Martyr, Queen Elizabeth, Mildred Cooke, Anne Cooke and Marjory Bowes, wife of John Knox.

137 Tillotson, J. *Lives of Illustrious Women of England* or *Biographical Treasury: containing memoirs of Royal, noble and celebrated British Females of the Past and Present Day.*

Thos. Holmes, London. Illustrated.

Eighteen queens and aristocrats in a chronological jumble, leavened by Mrs Bunyan, Charlotte Smith, Elizabeth Fry, 'the female Howard' and Mrs S. C. Hall, author of *Marian* (1840), a 'governess novel'.

1857

138 Anderson, Revd James. *Ladies of the Reformation – Memoirs of Distinguished Female Characters belonging to the period of the Reformation in the 16th Century – Germany, Switzerland, France, Italy and Spain.*

Blackie & Son, London and Edinburgh. Illustrated.

Sees Roman Catholic Church as Anti-Christ. Blames the suppression of the spirit of inquiry and consequent failure of the Reformation in Spain, Italy and much of France on persecution. Believes women to have been the great beneficiaries of the Reformation. 'For woman, in the present day, to read the Bible or to circulate Italian New Testaments in Italy, would be to land herself in a prison.' Includes Katharine von Bora Luther, Anna Zwingli, Idelette, Calvin, Marguerite de Valois, Jeanne D'Albret, Renée, Duchess of Ferrara, Olympia Morata and Leonor de Cisneros. Based on primary materials including documents of the Inquisition.

139 Adams, H. G. *Cyclopaedia of Female Biography consisting of Sketches of All Women who have been distinguished by great talents, strength of character, piety, benevolence, or moral virtue of any kind; forming a complete record of womanly excellence or ability.*

George Routledge, London. Reprinted 1869. 788pp.

A cheap British condensation of Hale (see entry 130), with some omissions and additions, for example all the Brontë sisters are there. But no index. Deeply shocked by Harriet Martineau's atheism and by George Sand's cross-dressing and socialism.

1858

140 Chambers, Robert. *Domestic Annals of Scotland from the Reformation to the Rebellion.*

W. and R. Chambers, Edinburgh and London. 2 volumes.

Interesting anecdotes. Includes Lady Abercorn, Lady Grizzel Baillie, Countess Bothwell, sixteenth-century calligrapher Esther Inglis, Mary, Queen of Scots, and many persecuted Scottish 'witches', for example Bessie Dunlop, Alison Peirson, Lady Foulis, Bessie Roy, Margaret Barclay, Margaret Wallace, Bessie Smith, Alison Dick, Agnes Finnie, Isobel Gowdie, Janet Braidhead, Jean Weir, Jonet and Margaret M'Lean, Katharine Liddell and Marion Purdie.

141 Clarke, Mary Cowden. *World-noted Women or Types of Womanly Attributes of all Lands and ages.*

D. Appleton and Co., New York. Illustrated.

Preface: 'This selection was made for me, not chosen by myself – far from all being looked upon as models, some instances are to be beheld as beacons of warning.' Mary Cowden Clarke 'remained above all, the spokesman and the eulogist of the female sex. ... A handsome, parlour-table vol. for the American public.' (Richard Altick, *The Cowden Clarkes*, OUP, 1948). Includes Sappho, Lucretia, Aspasia, Cleopatra, St Cecilia, Heloise, Laura, Valentine de Milan, Margaret of Anjou, Isabella of Castile (uncritically), Lady Jane Grey, Louise de La Vallière, Maria Theresa, Catherine II and Florence Nightingale.

26. The astronomer Caroline Herschel, from Adams' *Child-life and Girlhood of Remarkable Women*, 1883.

1859

142   Thomson, Katharine. *Celebrated Friendships*.

James Hogg and Sons, London. 2 volumes.

Preface: 'The writer has ... [dwelled] minutely on the incidents which are generally considered to be beneath the "dignity of history." ... It deals with those small facts of which life is made up.'

Includes: Magdalen Herbert and Dr Donne, Mrs Elizabeth Carter and Miss Talbot, Mrs Clive and David Garrick, Frances, Countess of Hertford and Henrietta Louisa, Countess of Pomfret, Mary Unwin and Cowper.

143   Anon. *Women of Worth – A Book for Girls*.

J. S. Virtue and Co., London. Illustrated. New edition 1886.

Again dependent on Hale, but emphasises the 'more commonplace people'. Quotes *Amos Barton* without acknowledgement. Then adds:

'It will be a good thing if this gathering of exemplary lives will teach some [girls] to study to be kind, and others to be quiet, and all to be cheerful.' Domestic ideology with a vengeance: Charlotte Brontë reduced to 'the worthy daughter', Elizabeth Fry to 'the Newgate schoolmistress', Lucy Hutchinson 'the pattern of domestic virtue', Mrs Wordsworth 'the poet's companion' and Lady Somerville 'the old-fashioned dame'. But also includes Sarah Martin, Sarah Judson, Mrs Barbauld, and Caroline Herschel.

Good illustrations for iconography of the collective biography of women.

144 Ellis, Sarah Stickney. *The Mothers of Great Men.*

London. Illustrated. New editions London 1874, Edinburgh 1883.

Influential author of best-selling works of Separate Spheres ideology:

Daughters of England, The Women of England, etc.

Includes Augustine, Wesley, Cowper and Byron, whose mother was blamed for his excesses.

145 *Ellet, Mrs E. F. *Women Artists in All Ages and Countries.*

London.

Preface: 'I do not know that any work on Female Artists, either grouping them or giving a general history of their productions has ever been published.' Acknowledges debt to 'that excellent periodical *The Englishwoman's Journal*' for biographies of Rosa Bonheur, Fauceau and Harriet Hosmer. Includes Maria Sybilla Merian, Maria Cosway and Fanny Corbeaux. Encyclopaedic, if superficial listing. Mentions Society of Female Artists in London 1857 and Barbara Leigh Smith Bodichon: 'an admirable writer [and] excellent artist'.

146 Clayton, Ellen. *Notable Women – Stories of their Lives and Characteristics. A Book for Young Ladies.*

Dean and Son, London. 1859–60. Later edition 1875.

Readable but bland essays; domestic ideology explicit in chapter headings: 'Lucy Hutchinson, the Perfect Wife', 'Elizabeth Bunyan, the faithful Helpmate' etc.

1860

147 Russell, William. *Extraordinary Women: their Girlhood and Early Years.*

Routledge, Warne and Routledge, London. Illustrated. 2nd edition 1870.

Includes Joan of Arc, Elizabeth Fry, Mme Roland, Queen Christina of Sweden, Lucy Hutchinson, Ann Boleyn, Lady Mary Wortley

Montagu, Mrs Siddons, Charlotte Corday, Margaret Fuller, Hester Stanhope, Catherine II of Russia, and Mrs Opie.

148 The author of *Magdalen Strafford. The Home Life of English Ladies in the XVII Century.*

Bell and Daldy, London.

Includes Mrs Evelyn, Lady Warwick (Mary Boyle), Margaret Baxter, Mrs Basire, Lady Anne Clifford, Margaret, Duchess of Newcastle and Katherine Philips.

149 Wharton, Grace and Philip. *Queens of Society.*

Harper Bros., NY and London. 2 volumes. Illustrated. Later editions 1861 and 1867.

Heavily Victorian judgemental. Includes Duchess of Marlborough, Mme Roland, Lady Mary Wortley Montagu, Georgiana, Duchess of Devonshire, L. E. L., Mme de Sévigné, Sydney Lady Morgan, Jane, Duchess of Gordon, Mme Récamier, Lady Hervey, Mme de Stael, Mrs Thrale Piozzi, Lady Caroline Lamb and Mrs Damer.

150 Johnson, Joseph. *Heroines of Our Time: being sketches of the Lives of Eminent Women, with examples of their benevolent works, truthful lives, and noble deeds.*

Darton and Co., London.

Dedicated to his mother 'who in the midst of humble circumstances and proscribed opportunities has ever been a true ministering woman'. Opening chapter 'Ministering Women' is a *locus classicus* for pious, sentimental yet implacable domestic ideology – re an unfilial daughter: 'Better, infinitely better, that such a one should have died in infancy than ... that she forget ... the natural guardians of her life.' Nevertheless, the Preface speaks of women's dormant energy and urges privileged women to 'leave their homes of ease and elegance and visit the cottages; cellars, and garrets'. And Johnson includes as 'Ministering heroines', in addition to Pocohontas, Miss Marsh, Florence Nightingale, Elizabeth Fry, Charlotte Brontë and Margaret Fuller, even Rosa Bonheur and Dr Elizabeth Blackwell, praising 'the [latter's] marvellous energy, strength of character [and] talents of this pioneer of her sex'. The author also wrote *Famous Boys.*

1861

151 *Owen, Mrs Octavius Freire. *The Heroines of Domestic Life.*

Routledge, Warne and Routledge, London.

Dedicated to Miss Angela Burdett Coutts, 'whose consistent and unostentatious philanthropy attests her appreciation of the virtues these pages exhibit.'

> No man or woman has a right to become a mere cipher in existence, and both are called upon to imitate Him who worked 'unceasingly for all.' ... An invidious desire to restrict woman's legitimate influence, is no new thing; and although the universal increase of education confessedly demands her proportionate advancement, to keep pace with the day, we find narrow prejudice still striving to depress her in the social scale. ... The real answer ... to those casuists who impugn whatever may lead woman out of that inane repose in which they seek to keep her, is derived from the facts themselves ... domestic heroism desires not fame, which is alien to its very nature; yet becomes of public import, as its unassuming virtue spreads from the cottage to the throne, cheers the home or the hospital, and alleviates even the scaffold and the gaol. ... [It] cannot be denied that association with aspects of severer duty, is apt to give a masculine hardness to the mind and the manners, inauspicious to feminine delicacy. .... The constant habit of thinking for herself, of ruling rather than obeying, nay, even conversance with subjects of hospital and camp life, wears off from woman ... her soft and gentle character. Our observation may be thought strange; but we think that such heroines never proved their claim to the appellation more, than when they voluntarily sacrificed the attractiveness of feminine sensibility, by the exercise of self-imposed obnoxious offices.

> Graver thoughts of [woman's] true destiny, must be imparted into the old system of educating her to be merely a pretty puppet in the drawing-room. The author hopes to 'teach woman to endure – her chief lesson in life! – and unselfishly to support others – her main prerogative!

A Christian feminist. Includes: Ruth, Antigone, Margaret Roper, Anne Askew, Pocohontas, Lucy Hutchinson, Lady Rachel Russell, Grizel Cochrane, Winifred, Countess of Nithsdale, Helen Walker (i.e. Jeannie Deans), Flora Macdonald, Elizabeth Fry, Sarah Martin, Grace Darling and Florence Nightingale.

152 Holt, Emily Sarah. *Memoirs of Royal Ladies.*

2 volumes.

Preface: 'Of the ten royal ladies in these volumes, with one exception, no memoirs have ever before been written in English.'

Includes Ela, Countess of Salisbury, d. 1261, Alicia de Lacy, d. 1348, Joan of Kent, d. 1385 and Jane Beaufort, d. 1444.

153 Williams, Jane. *The Literary Women of England: Includes a biographical epitome of all the most eminent to the year 1700 and sketches of the poetesses to the year 1850.*

London.

Moralistic, prescriptive and narrowly religious. 'Aphra Behn is the first English authoress whose life was openly wrong, and whose writings were obscene.' Refers to Mrs Manley's 'disgraceful tales' in her *New Atlantis*. Centilevre was 'strongly tinctured with the indelicacy of her time'. Substantial panegyrics on Hannah More, Felicia Hemans and L. E. L. Anti-Rousseauist: 'Reverie is not allowable.' Her sources include Wilford, Ballard, Granger, Walpole, Craik, Hale and Chambers (see entries 32, 38, 48, 43, 121, 130 and 140 respectively). (See also Margaret Ezell in entry 38).

154 *Clayton, Ellen. *Women of the Reformation. Their Lives, Faith and Trials*.

Dean and Son, London. Illustrated.

Heavily partisan Protestant feminism. Preface: 'Every true Protestant heart must glow with sympathy and admiration for the Women who ... gave their lives ... to the cause of the Reformation.' A racier retelling of Anderson (1855), without acknowledgement. Highlights Anne Boleyn, Catherine Parr, Anne Askew, Katherine Willoughby, Duchess of Suffolk, Anne Cooke and Ann Hooper.

155 *Hill, Matthew Davenport. *Our Exemplars, Poor and Rich* or *Biographical Sketches of Men and Women who have, by an extraordinary use of their opportunities benefited their fellow-creatures*.

London. New edition, with additions, 1880.

Socially radical, secular feminism by friend of Barbara Leigh Smith Bodichon. Includes working-class Irishwoman Bridget Burke, rescuer of young girls in Dublin, the washerwoman Catherine Wilkinson, community nurse in Liverpool cholera epidemic, and the African-American Abolitionist Sarah Remond's own account of her struggle for an education in North American States: 'Prejudice against colour has always been the one thing above all others, which has cast its gigantic shadow over my whole life.' Brougham's Introduction acknowledges Craik (1847, see entry 121). 'Notices of self-made women are rare in [Smiles' book *Self-help*] an omission which is disappointing, and which assuredly does not arise from any scarcity of materials.' Davenport Hill is in 'Self-help' tradition but with the emphasis on helping oneself in order to be able to help others. Mary Carpenter asked not to be included.

1862

156 *Kavanagh, Julia. *English Women of Letters; biographical sketches*.

Leipzig. 2 volumes. Another edition London, 1863.

From Aphra Behn to Lady Morgan, including Sarah Fielding, Charlotte Smith, Fanny Burney, Edgeworth, and Opie, i.a. Finds Behn offensive except for *Oronooko*: 'She sank woman to the level of man's coarseness'. Lively discussion of Inchbald, cool re Austen's lack of Charlotte Brontë's 'passionate eloquence'. Strong statement on socialized gender difference as based on more than educational disparity:

> It is not the Greek and Latin of boys that gives them a future advantage over their more ignorant sisters. It is that they are trained to act a part in life, and a part worth acting, whilst girls are either taught to look on life, or, worse still, told how to practise its light and unworthy arts.

157   *Kavanagh, Julia. *French Women of Letters, Biographical Sketches.*

London. 2 volumes.

Preface: 'The novel is not merely the great feature of modern literature, it is also the only branch in which women have acquired undisputed eminence. . . . [J. K. aims to rescue] from forgetfulness the labours and the names once honoured and celebrated of other women.' Herself a novelist, Kavanagh gives close, ethical criticism to the work of Mlle de Gournay, Mme de Scudéry, Mme de Lafayette, Mme de Genlis, and Mme de Stael, i.a., but no George Sand – because she was still alive?

158   Yonge, Charlotte (ed.). *Biographies of Good Women.*

C. Mozley, London. 1862–5. 2 volumes.

Collected from *The Monthly Packet*, i.e. intended for adolescent girls. Christian anti-feminist: 'We have described the Sufferers – the Learners – the Workers. . . . The diamond of perfect womanhood has many facets, and thro' all the light of Heaven is reflected. . . . But the light of Heaven it must be. All the women of our biographies . . . were alike in this one matter – that their faith . . . was the brightness of their lives.'

Includes Lucy Hutchinson, Lady Russell, the black slave Mum Bett, Elizabeth Carter, Elizabeth Smith, Hannah More, Elizabeth Fry, Anna Gurney, La Mère Angelique, Mrs Trimmer, Dorothy Words-worth, and Sophia Swetchine.

159   Chorley, Henry. *Thirty Years' Musical Recollections.*

Hurst and Blackett, London. 2 volumes. With portraits. Another edition, introduced by Ernest Newman, 1926.

The author was music critic of *The Athenaeum*.

Includes: Mmes Alboni, Bosio, Grisi, Malibran, Mme Pasta, Persiana, Rachel, Henrietta Sontag, Pauline Viardot and Jenny Lind.

27. The singer Pauline Viardot Garcia; frontispiece to Clayton's *Queens of Song*, 1863.

160 Anderson, Revd James. *Memorable Women of the Puritan Times. 1603–1688.*

Blackie & Son, London. 2 volumes.

Includes Brilliana Conway, Anne Bradstreet, Mary Dyer, Quaker victim of Puritan persecution, all the Cromwell family women, Margaret Baxter, Elizabeth Bunyan, Lady Rachel Russell, and two impassioned chapters on the martyrdom of Alice, Lady Lisle and of Elizabeth Gaunt.

1863

161 *Clayton, Ellen. *Queens of Song ... from the earliest days of opera to the present.*

Smith, Elder and Co., London. 2 volumes. With six portraits.

Dedicated to Mme Viardot Garcia.

An interesting historical overview with excellent list of sources. Does justice to the contribution of Jewish women singers. Includes: Katherine Tofts, Anastasia Robinson, Francesca Cuzzoni, Elizabeth Billington, Angelica Catalani, Giuditta Pasta, Henrietta Sontag, Maria Malibran, Pauline Viardot Garcia, Clara Novello and Jenny Lind.

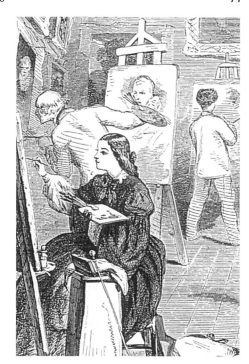

28. Fanny Corbeaux painting in the National Gallery, from Johnson's *Clever Girls of our time and how they became Famous Women*, 1863.

162

Johnson, Joseph. *Clever Girls of our time and how they became Famous Women – whose lives furnish an incentive and encouragement to effort and endurance; and whose example stimulates to industry and perseverance.*

3rd edition. Gall and Inglis, London. Illustrated. Went into 8 editions. Last edition 1903.

Preface respects girls who concentrate on music, singing or painting as a means to a livelihood: 'That girl who has resolved upon self-dependence, and who is intensely absorbed in self-culture as the means to self-maintenance, presents one of the most cheering sights in all this world.' Includes Clara Novello, the Hon. Mrs Norton, Harriet Hosmer, Ida Pfeiffer, Elizabeth Carter, Elizabeth Smith, polymath, Catherine Macaulay, Elizabeth Barrett, Catherine Hayes, Malibran, Fanny Corbeaux and Agnes Strickland. George Eliot is a significant absentee.

1864

163 Russell, W., LL.D. *Eccentric Personages.*

Misogynist sneering assessment of Lady Mary Wortley Montagu, Amazon Snell, Lady Hester Stanhope, Mme de Genlis and Margaret Fuller.

1. Madame Rolland. 2. Charlotte Corday. 3. Marguerite of Anjou. 4. Madame d'Arblay. 5. Grace Darling; 6. Madame Pfeiffer. 7. Joan of Arc. 8. Josephine; 9. Lady Jane Grey. 10. Mary Queen of Scots 11. Maria Theresa of Austria. 12. Lady Rachel Russell. 13. Lady Arabella Stuart. 14. Marie Antoinette. 15. Mrs. Hemans

29. Frontispiece to *Fifty Famous Women*, 1864.

164 Anderson, William. *The Scottish Nation* or *the Surnames, Families, Literature, Honours and Biographical History of the People of Scotland.*

A. Fullarton and Co., Edinburgh and London. 3 volumes. c. 2400 pp.

The Preface makes it clear that the 'People of Scotland' are her sons; the very few non-sons included are Joanna Baillie, Mary Brunton, Alicia Cockburn, Agnes, Countess of Dunbar and March, Mrs Anne Grant of Laggan, Flora Macdonald, Mary, Queen of Scots, Susan Ferrier and Christian Isobel Johnstone 'one of the most esteemed of modern female novelists'.

165 Anon. *Fifty Famous Women. Their Virtues and Failings and the Lessons of their Lives.*

Ward, Lock and Tyler, London.

Promises Separate Spheres' anti-feminism. Introduction: 'From a great many kinds of work, women are necessarily debarred by their own constitution, and that of society, and equally by the universal law which, in a crowded labour-market, thrusts out the weaker until the stronger are fully supplied.' Therefore this author singles out women 'who have worked to do their duty'. But in fact the selection of lives is much more inspiriting and heroic than the Introduction suggests. No historical logic followed in the sequence of the 50 who include: Swift's Stella, Charlotte Corday, Anne Askew, Mme Roland, Grace Darling, Lucy Hutchinson, Mme de Stael, Ida Pfeiffer, Pocohontas, Mrs Chisholm, Charlotte Brontë, Elizabeth Fry, Mrs Hemans, Frederika Bremer and Cowper's Mrs Unwin.

166 Adams, W. H. D. *Famous Beauties and Historic Women.*

C. J. Skeet, London.

Rightly called 'a miscellaneous writer' by the *DNB*, the author here embarks on his career as a one-man factory of popular collective biography for the next 30 years.

Preface: 'Simply light gossiping anecdotal sketches'.

Includes Nell Gwynn, Duchess of Cleveland, Elizabeth Hamilton, Mrs Radcliffe – 'the first novelist who employed fear and terror' – Mme de Stael, Agnes Sorel, and Mme Récamier.

167 Wilson, Revd William. *Heroines of the Household.*

Pious, non-feminist domestic ideology praising the 'work of some of the noblest specimens of Christian womanhood ... intended as illustrious of woman's sphere and influence.' Includes Monica, mother of Augustine, Olympia Morata, Italian Protestant 'brilliant star of the Reformation', Lady Brilliana Conway, French lady-founders of Sisterhoods (e.g. Mme de Chantal), Grisell Hume Lady Baillie, Mary Ann Galton, Mrs Schimmelpenninck, the Kaiserswerth Deaconesses and Miss Marsh's labours among the navvies.

1865

168 Menzies, Sutherland, i.e. Elizabeth Stone. *Royal Favourites.*

John Maxwell and Co., London. 2 volumes.

Includes both royal mistresses of kings, e.g. Agnes Sorel, Diane de Poitiers and Gabrielle D'Estrée, and the court favourites of queens – of Elizabeth Tudor, Mary, Queen of Scots, Marie de Medici, Anne of Denmark, Anne of Austria, and Catherine II of Russia.

169 Brightwell, Celia. *Above Rubies – Memorials of Christian Gentlewomen.*

T. Nelson and Sons, London. Later edition 1882.

Preface: 'Many of these – my favourite heroines – have not, indeed, been distinguished for remarkable deeds of courage or daring; but all were kind-hearted and true, firm friends, and exemplary in the discharge of domestic duties.' Includes Mme Guizot, Caroline Perthes (daughter of poet Claudius also mentioned in Wilson (entry 167)), Mrs Grant of Laggan, Mme Necker, Lady Fanshawe, Winifred Countess of Nithsdale, Queen Louisa of Prussia, Susanna Wesley (including an inaccurate account of her daughter Mehetabel Wesley Wright), Katharine von Bora Luther and Lucy Hutchinson.

1866

170 *Parkes, Bessie (ed.). *Vignettes* – [12 Biographical Sketches from] *The Englishwoman's Journal.*

London.

Feminist insistence on women's diversity by editor of *The Englishwoman's Journal* financed by women's rights leader Barbara Bodichon. Preface: 'There is a moral in their utter dissimilarity which I leave to the intelligent reader.' Includes Mme Luce, pioneer teacher of Algerian girls, Mme Pape Carpentier, Anna Jameson, Mrs Delany, Dr Harriot Hunt, Mme Swetchine, Mme de Lamartine, and Miss Bosanquet, i.a.

1867

171 Adams, W. H. D. *The Sunshine of Domestic Life.* [Later editions titled *Stories of the Lives of Noble Women.*]

T. Nelson and Sons, London. Later editions 1904 and 1911 as part of Nelson's Girls' Library.

Unbelievably saccharine and infantilizing first choice of title for the stories of the martyrs and heroines Anne Askew, Alice Lisle, Elizabeth Gaunt, Lady Jane Grey, Mme Roland and Charlotte Brontë, i.a.

Preface: 'It is well that these examples should be kept before the eyes of the younger female members of our families; and that they should be encouraged to aspire to a high standard of duty, while not forgetting that their true happiness will always lie within the home circle.'

1868

172 Martineau, Harriet. *Biographical Sketches.*

London. 4th edition enlarged, with autobiographical sketch, 1876.

Collection of obituaries previously published in *The Daily News*.

Includes Charlotte Brontë, Amelia Opie, Mary Russell Mitford, Mrs Marcet, Mrs Wordsworth, Mrs Jameson, the Misses Berry and the Abolitionist, Lady Noel Byron.

173 Strickland, Agnes and Elizabeth. *Lives of the Tudor Princesses, including Lady Jane Gray and her sisters.*

Longmans and Co., London. Revised edition 1888.

Again a serious historical study based on original archival research.

Includes Lady Eleanor Brandon, Lady Margaret Clifford and Lady Arabella Stuart by Agnes Strickland; Princess Mary Tudor, the Duchess of Suffolk, Lady Jane Gray, Lady Katharine Gray, and Lady Mary Gray [sic], by Elizabeth Strickland.

1869

174 Russell, W. Clark. *Representative Actors. A Collection of Criticisms, Anecdotes, Personal Descriptions from the 16th to the Present Century.*

Chandos Library, F. Warne and Co., London. 1869–81. 17 volumes.

A useful companion to the British theatre. Dedicated to Miss Helen Faucit. An underused source for women's stage-history.

175 *Stanton, Elizabeth Cadey *et al. Eminent Women of the Age.* [American].

S. M. Betts and Co., Hartford, Conn. Illustrated.

Strongly feminist. Includes section by Elizabeth Cady Stanton on women in the Women's Rights Movement in the USA – Sarah and Angelina Grimké, Lucretia Mott, Frances Gage, Lucy Stone, Susan B. Anthony and others. Other entries on Harriet Beecher Stowe, Dr med. Elizabeth Blackwell, Dr med. Harriot Hunt, Harriet Hosmer, Rosa Bonheur, Helen Faucit and Julia Ward Howe.

1871

176 Mossman, Samuel. *Gems of Womanhood or Sketches of Distinguished Women in various ages and nations.*

Gall and Inglis, London and Edinburgh.

Examples for 'the rising female generation'.

Preface: 'As a rule … the women who have been most remarkable in their public career, were those whose youthful training was of the most feminine character. Even the most courageous … were generally of the most retiring and domestic character in youth . . . and retired again into modest obscurity.' Includes Joan of Arc, Octavia, Zenobia, Boadicea, Flora Macdonald, Elizabeth Fry, Grace Darling, African women who succoured Mungo Park, Letitia Landon, Anne Damer, Mme de Stael, Elizabeth Montagu, Mary, Countess of Pembroke, Mrs Hemans, Mme de Sévigné, Lady Rachel Russell, Anne Askew and Mme Guyon.

177   Hall, Mr and Mrs S. C. *A Book of Memories of Great Men and Women of the Age, from Personal Acquaintance.*

London. 2nd edition 1877.

Pious, anti-feminist. Written in old age:

> I am quite sure; the leading . . . impulse of women is to render themselves agreeable and helpful to men; . . . in spite of the 'strong-minded'. . . . [A] masculine woman is more repulsive than an effeminate man . . . outraging the declared will of God. A woman without an Altar is even more degraded than a woman without a Hearth.

Contrasts contemporary sensationalist women novelists, contaminated by 'a degraded woman of genius . . . from France', (presumably George Sand), with the morally healthy Hannah More, Maria Edgeworth, Amelia Opie, Lady Morgan, Felicia Hemans, Frederika Bremer, L. E. L. and Mary Russell Mitford. Also includes Barbara Hogland, Grace Aguilar, Catherine Sinclair, and Jane and Anna Maria Porter.

178   Brightwell, Cecilia. *Memorial Chapters in the Lives of Christian Gentlewomen.*

Book Society, 28 paternoster Row, London. 1871–3.

Preface: 'This little book is designed for the instruction and entertainment of youthful readers, especially of young girls just entering upon the more serious duties of womanhood.'

Another Protestant portrait collection. Includes Presbyterian Lady Colquhoun, Mrs Schimmelpenninck, Miss Bosanquet, Margaret Fuller d'Ossoli, Olympia Morata, Jane Taylor, author of 'Twinkle, twinkle little star', and Katherine von Bora Luther. The author also wrote *Memorials of Mrs Opie*.

179   Tytler, Sarah, i.e. Keddie, Henrietta and Watson, J. L. *The Songstresses of Scotland.*

London. 2 volumes.

Preface: 'The object is to bring together into one group some gifted women [poets] whose songs are known wherever the Scotch foot treads or the Scotch language lingers . . . alike in the kitchen and the ha'.'

1872

180 Strickland, Agnes. *Lives of the last four Princesses of the Royal House of Stuart.*

Bell and Daldy, London.

Includes Mary, eldest daughter of Charles I, Elizabeth his second daughter, and Henrietta the youngest. Also Louisa, daughter of James II. Based on archival research in The Hague, the Bodleian Library and Lambeth Palace.

181 Gould, S. Baring. *Lives of the Saints.*

John Hodges, London. 1872–89. 17 volumes.

Compiled by Anglican Divine who wrote 'Onward Christian Soldiers'. A new edition revised with introduction and additional lives of English martyrs, Cornish and Welsh saints, etc. in 16 volumes 1897–8.

1873

182 Menzies, Sutherland, i.e. Stone, Elizabeth. *Political Women.*

Henry S. King and Co., London. 2 volumes.

Author an anti-feminist writer of history textbooks for school-children. Introduction: 'In selecting the careers of certain celebrated women who have flung themselves with ardour into the vortex of politics, the author's choice has ... [centred] on the most conspicuous arena; when Peace and War, crowns and dynasties, have trembled in the balance, and even the fate of a nation has been at stake. [But] it will be seen that the fierce contention has commonly involved the sacrifice of conjugal happiness, the welfare of children, domestic peace, reputation, and all the amenities of the gentle life. If clever women obtain the influence of men, they cannot expect to retain the influence of women ... Fortunately in [English] political history, the instances are rare of women who have quitted the sphere of domesticity to take an active part in the affairs of state.' Stone opposes the 'agitators for women's rights, preferring the preservation of women's gentleness, purity and refinement'.

Volume I includes Anne de Bourbon, Duchesse de Longueville, Duchesse de Chevreuse, Anne of Austria, Duchesse de Montbauzon and Duchesse de Chatillon, the Princess Palatine. Volume II includes Mlle de Montpensier, Princesse des Ursins, the Duchess of Marlborough and Queen Anne.

183 Hall, Spencer, 'The Sherwood Forester'. *Biographical Sketches of Remarkable People, chiefly from Personal Recollection.*

The author is the mesmerist who cured Harriet Martineau.

His Chapter 13 'Self-devoted women' mingles the famous and the wholly obscure: Florence Nightingale, Mary Russell Mitford, Nancy Shacklock, Phoebe Howitt and Jane Jerram.

1874

184 Redgrave, Samuel. *A Dictionary of Artists of the English School. Painters, Sculptors, architects, engravers and ornamentalists with notices of their lives and works.*

London. New edition revised to the present date by Miss F. M. Redgrave, with a biographical sketch of the compiler, London, 1878.

Not indexed but invaluable. Covers, critically but not unsympathetically, c.70 women artists from mid-seventeenth century until those dead by 1860. Mostly miniaturist painters, flower painters, watercolourists. Many of them daughters, sisters or wives of male artists.

Includes: Mary Beale, Elizabeth Blackwell, Maria Cosway, Anne Damer, Mrs Delany, Gentileschi, Angelica Kauffmann, Anne Mee, Mary Moser, Katherine Read, Frances Reynolds (who 'does not, indeed, seem to have met with much encouragement'), Olive Serres, Mrs Sharples, Sarah Siddons, Maria Verelst and Patience Wright. An important underused source.

185 Anon. *Women of History by eminent writers.*

William P. Nimmo, London and Edinburgh. Illustrated.

Companion volume to *Men of History*. Includes short extracts on Sappho, Aspasia, Hypatia, Joan of Arc, Margaret, Duchess of Newcastle, Pocohontas, Noor Mahal, Katherine Philips, Lady Fanshawe, Mary Astell, Lady Mary Wortley Montagu, Mrs Barbauld, Hannah More, Elizabeth Inchbald, Mary Brunton, Caroline Herschel, Sarah Siddons and Charlotte Brontë, among others. No sources for the eminent writers' texts on these women.

186 Ritchie, Thackeray Anne. *A Book of Sibyls.*

Smith, Elder and Co., London.

Thackeray's daughter, and sister-in-law of Leslie Stephen. A tribute to outstanding women writers, especially Mrs Barbauld, Miss Edgeworth, Mrs Opie, Jane Austen and Mrs Gaskell, the last with personal recollections. Dedicated to Mrs Oliphant, 'a dear Sibyl of our own'.

30. Elizabeth Gaskell by Samuel Laurence, 1854.

1875

187 Clayton, Ellen. *Celebrated Women – stories of their Lives and Example, literary, social and historical. A Book for Young Ladies.*

Dean and Son, London.

Heavily Christian domestic ideology: includes Margaret Baxter, Elizabeth Burnet, Susanna Wesley, Elizabeth Smith, Charlotte Brontë and also interesting stories of unsung heroines like Charlotte Elizabeth Browne, the blind activist for the blind, and Phela Tonna, teacher of the deaf-mute.

188 Bruce, Charles (ed.). *The Book of Noble Englishwomen Lives made illustrious by heroism, goodness and great attainments.*

W. P. Nimmo, London and Edinburgh.

Eclectic use of material admitted to be taken from Kavanagh, Yonge, Bessie Parkes, and Mrs S. C. Hall (see entries 156, 158, 170 and 177 respectively).

189 Humphrey, Mrs E. J. *Gems of India* or *Sketches of Distinguished Hindoo and Mahomedan Women.* [American.]

Nelson and Phillips, New York.

Dedicated to 'American women of whatever religious denomination ... with the prayer that ... interest in the women of heathen lands may be greatly increased'.

Sanjogata, Pudmunee, Durgaveatee, Jodh Baiee, Chand Sultana, Noor Mahal, Mumtaz Mahal, Ahuliya Baiee, Kishna Comara Baie, Ranee of Jhansi, the Begums of Bhopal and last chapter on 'The women of India'. Christian missionary perspective.

190 Weitbrecht, Mrs. *The Women of India and Christian Work in the Zenana.*

James Nisbet, London.

Preface: 'Every effort we can make to impress our country-people with the importance of helping to raise the women of our Indian Empire to their right position is worth making. ... Those who desire continuous information on the subject of this book, will find it in *The Female Missionary Intelligencer* [and] in *The Indian Female Evangelist*.' Includes Hannah Marshman, Harriet Winslow, Mary Anne Wilson, Mary Bird, Margaret Wilson, Louisa Mundy, Charlotte Haberlin, Hannah Mullens, Louisa Gomez and Alice Wade who worked as educationalists among girls in India between 1800 and 1871.

191 *Johnson, Joseph. *Brave Women: who have been distinguished for Heroic Actions and Noble Virtues; who have exhibited fearless courage; stout hearts; and intrepid resolve.*

Gall and Inglis, Edinburgh and London.

Preface: 'Woman, in courage, in resolution, in purpose, is man's equal, often his superior. ... Combines domestic ideology *and* public sphere feminism: the bravery of woman is best seen and developed at home. ... [But] the power to occupy positions of public trust, in any emergency, is the right and title to such occupation. Hence we would have the education of woman more general.' Includes Ann Flaxman, Ann Cobbett, Félicie de Fauveau, Henrietta Feller and Hester Lane, as well as Joan of Arc, Ann Askew, Isabel Brown, Flora Macdonald, Mme Roland and Grace Darling.

1876

192 *Clayton, Ellen. *English Female Artists.*

Tinsley Bros., London. 2 volumes.

Very useful reference work with excellent listings of works by the artists and of art history sources consulted. More detailed than Ellet (see entry 145); interesting appreciation of Barbara Bodichon as landscape artist and feminist, and an illuminating short section on her own modest career as children's book illustrator before turning to writing the collective biography of women.

193 Spears, Robert. *Record of Unitarian Worthies.*

31. Emily Osborn's missing portrait of the painter and feminist Barbara Bodichon from a photo in Helen Blackburn's *Record of Women's Suffrage*, 1902.

E. T. Whitfield, London. Later revised edition of this work is *Memorable Unitarians*, 1906.

Includes under 'Distinguished Women': Lucy Aikin, Sarah Austin, Joanna Baillie, Mrs Barbauld, Lady Byron, Mrs Cappe, founder of Sunday Schools and autobiographer, Catherine Wilkinson of Liverpool, Miss Gifford, Mrs Marcet, Mrs Hughes, Mrs Rayner, Helen Maria Williams, Mrs Priestley, and Mrs Gaskell.

1877

194 Murch, Revd Jerom. *Mrs Barbauld and her Contemporaries – Sketches of Some Eminent Literary and Scientific Englishwomen.*

Longman Green, London.

Originally papers given to the Bath Institution by local Unitarian Divine. Principally devoted to Mrs Barbauld and based on Lucy Aikin, but includes interesting notes on Hannah More, Joanna Baillie, Mary Somerville and Caroline Herschel.

32. The mathematician
Mary Somerville;
frontispiece to Balfour's
Women worth emulating,
1877.

195 *Balfour, Mrs Clara Lucas. *Women worth emulating.*

Sunday School Union, London.

Preface: 'Emulation is the spirit most desirable to arouse in the young
... the following varied selections of womanly worth and wisdom are
presented to the young *of their own sex* [my emphasis] in the hope
that studious habits, intellectual pursuits, domestic industry and
sound religious principles may be promoted and confirmed.'

She includes the childhood and adult lives of Mary Somerville,
Caroline Herschel, Charlotte Elliott, writer of the hymn 'Just as I am
without one plea', Elizabeth Smith, Amelia Opie and Sarah Martin as
all worthy of emulation in their combination of womanliness and
outstanding achievement. Note frontispiece of Mary Somerville as
Emile-like, untutored child of nature before she began on self-
motivated study.

196 Blackburne, E. Owens. *Illustrious Irishwomen, being Memoirs of the
most noted Irishwomen from the earliest Ages to the Present Century.*

Tinsley Bros., London. 2 volumes.

Preface: 'To preserve in a collected form the names and achievements
of some of the more gifted daughters of Erin, has been the silent
patriotism of my life. ... This is the *first* time a work of this kind –

dealing solely with memoirs of Irishwomen – has been attempted. There is a good deal of original matter ... some hitherto unpublished poems by William Wordsworth, and the *true* history of the romantic friendship of the "Ladies of Llangollen".' Acknowledges help of Julia Grierson, Ellen Clayton and Lady Wilde.

Volume I: Queen Macha, Queen Meave, Saint Brigit, Dearbhforguill, Margaret O'Carroll, Grainne O'Mailly and the actresses Peg Woffington, Mrs Bellamy, Mrs Robinson, Kitty Clive, Dorothy Jordan, Elizabeth Farren, Maria Pope, Miss O'Neill and Catherine Hayes.

Volume II: 'Literary Women': Susanna Centilevre, Constantia Grierson, Charlotte Brooke, Mary Tighe, Maria Edgeworth, Felicia Hemans, Sydney Lady Morgan, Countess of Blessington, Caroline Norton and the Ladies of Llangollen.

Sources include Miss Cusack's *History of Ireland*, P. Fitzgerald's *Lives of the Kembles*, Mrs Delany's *Memoirs*, Miss Berry's *Journal*, Ellen Clayton's *Queens of Song*, Griswold's *Female Poets*, S. C. Hall's *Memories*, Ballard, Hale, Doran and Alibone, i.a.

197   Walford, Edward. *Tales of our great families.*

London. 1877–80. 4 volumes. New edition 1890.

The higher gossip. Includes: the two fair Gunnings, the three Miss Walpoles, Lady Hester Stanhope, the Ladies of Llangollen and the Hon. Mrs Damer.

1878

198   Chambers, W. *Stories of Remarkable Persons.*

W. and R. Chambers, London.

Includes Caroline Herschel, Mary Somerville, Dorothy Wordsworth, Sarah Martin and Miss Stirling Graham.

199   Webb, Alfred. *A Compendium of Irish Biography.*

M. H. Gill and Son, Dublin.

Overwhelmingly male but includes St Bridget, Constantia Grierson, Kitty Clive, Mrs Bellamy, Laetitia Pilkington, Swift's Stella and Vanessa, Peg Woffington, Frances Sheridan, Mrs Delany, Elizabeth O'Neill, Anne Devlin, Lady Dufferin, Grace O'Malley, Lady Morgan, Catherine McAuley, Lola Montez and Julia Kavanagh. No Anna Wheeler or Fanny or Anna Parnell. Gives sources.

200   Adams, W. H. D. *Women of Fashion and Representative women in Letters and Society.*

Tinsley Bros., London. 2 volumes.

Volume I: Lady Mary Wortley Montagu, Duchess of Marlborough, Lady Morgan and Miss Berry. Volume 2: Mme D'Arblay, Elizabeth Inchbald, Countess of Blessington, Charlotte Brontë and Harriet Martineau (shocked by her 'miserable creed of agnosticism'.)

201 Yonge, C. D. Professor. *The Seven Heroines of Christendom.*

Chilworth, London.

Joan of Arc, Margaret of Anjou, Isabella of Castile, Charlotte, Countess of Derby, Maria Theresa, Flora Macdonald and Marie-Antoinette.

1879

202 Read, Charles. *The Cabinet of Irish Literature – Selections from the works of the chief poets, orators, and prose writers of Ireland, with biographical sketches and literary notices.*

Blackie & Sons, London. 4 volumes.

Organized chronologically. Volume I includes Mary Monk, Susanna Centilevre, Constantia Grierson, Laetitia Pilkington, Frances Sheridan and Charlotte Brooke.

Volume II includes Elizabeth Ryves, Mary Tighe, Mary Leadbeater, Maria Edgeworth and the Countess of Blessington.

Volume III includes Sydney Lady Morgan.

Volume IV, edited by T. P. O'Connor, includes Mrs S. C. Hall, Lady Wilde, Julia Kavanagh, Frances Power Cobbe, Eva Mary Kelly, Ellen Downing, Mrs Alexander, Frances Brownes, Mrs Cashel Hoey, Rosa Mulholland, E. Owens Blackburne, Mrs Caffan, Margaret Stokes and Mrs J. H. Riddell. But no Fanny Parnell.

203 Clayton, Ellen. *Female Warriors – Memorials of Female Valour and Heroism, from the Mythological Ages to the Present Era.*

Tinsley Bros., London. 2 volumes.

Ranges from mythological Amazons to contemporary women warriors in Dahomey and Southern Africa. Includes Semiramis, Artemisia, Cleopatra, Boadicea, Zenobia, Arab warrior queens, Eleanor of Aquitaine, Blanche of Castile, Agnes Dunbar, Joan of Arc, Margaret of Anjou, Isabella of Castile, Louise Labé, Mary, Queen of Scots, Elizabeth I, Christina of Sweden, Mary Anne Talbot, Noor Mahal, and Lukshmi Baiee, the Ranee of Jhansi, among many others. Again a very useful listing of sources.

204 Groves, G. (ed.). *Dictionary of Music and Musicians.*

Macmillan and Co., London. 1879–90. 4 volumes and index volume.

Includes Marianne and Cecilia Davies, Cuzzoni, Malibran, Susannah
Cibber, Anastasia Robinson, Mme Vestris, Mrs Mounsey, Fanny
Davies, Clara Novello, Jenny Lind, Pauline Viardot, Clara Schu-
mann, Henriette Voigt, Catalani, Paton, Grisi, Tietjens and Patti.
Mostly great singers, therefore, with a few instrumentalists. Women
as composers hardly noted.

1880

205 *Betham-Edwards, M. *Six Life studies of Famous Women.*

Griffith and Farran, London.

The author is the novelist niece of Matilda Betham (see entry 75) and
friend of Barbara Bodichon and George Eliot.

Preface: 'Young readers read short biographies, or none at all. ...
[My] object ... is rather to popularize less known memories of
remarkable persons than to abridge those already famous. ... It is
impossible not to [regret] the glorious women of all ages and
countries about whom next to nothing is known ... e.g. Polla
Argentaria, wife of Lucan ... the Renaissance printers Mmes
Estienne, or Fielding's gifted and learned sister Sarah – we do not
know what became of her. ... Women philanthropists and scholars,

33. Matilda Betham-
Edwards in Helen C.
Black's *Notable Women
Authors of the Day*,
1893.

social reformers and artists, educationalists and romancers, all fare alike. History has no time for them.' Includes Caroline Herschel, Elizabeth Carter, Matilda Betham, Mme Pape Carpentier, Alexandrine Tinne, and Fernan Caballero, all of whom prized knowledge and thought and 'lead us beyond the narrow vision and limited aims of every-day existence'.

206 Adams, W. H. D. *Woman's Work and Worth in Girlhood, Maidenhood and Wifehood, with hints on self-culture etc.*

John Hogg, London. An abridged edition, with illustrations published as *Exemplary Women*, 1882.

Extraordinary lucky dip of unchronological biographical anecdotage re Woman as Mother, Woman in the World of Art, Woman as Heroine etc. Then two useful chapters of factual information re entry requirements for girls into higher education and employment openings for educated women, ranging from pharmacy to printing and horticulture.

207 Darton, John Maw. *Famous Girls who have become Illustrious Women.*

Collingridge City Press, London. 17th edition. Date of 1st edition unknown.

Pious, sentimental, anodyne, and chronologically haywire. Includes Caroline Chisholm and Lydia Child and the 'trying circumstances' of Laura Bridgman, blind, deaf and dumb. Mentions Frederika Bremer without her feminism and Harriet Martineau without her atheism.

208 Smith, George. *Short History of Christian Missions from Abraham and Paul to Carey, Livingstone and Duff.*

T. and T. Clark, Edinburgh. 8 editions.

Women given three pages out of 243.

Mentions Mary Seelye, MD in Calcutta, and Janet Colquhoun Smith, Mrs Marshman, Mrs Wilson, Mrs Margaret Wilson, Mrs Anderson and Mrs Braidwood, all starting up schools and orphanages in India in the early nineteenth century.

209 *Pitman, Emma Raymond. *Heroines of the Mission Field. Biographical Sketches.*

Cassell, Petter, Galpin and Co., London.

Preface: 'These holy, useful women for the most part laboured in obscurity, suffered in obscurity, and died in obscurity. ... I have gathered up the fragments of biographical lore, scattered here and there, to collect memorials from surviving friends, to examine documents, volumes and journals ... to honour the names and works of these missionary labourers. ... Missionary life ... loses its glamour when pursued far away in lonely deserts, by drought-stricken plains, tiger and serpent-haunted jungles, on frozen icebergs, or upon [a] solitary isle. ... Faith, works, danger, and pathos, are so strangely mingled, that one stands conscience-stricken at one's own littleness, when compared with these self-denying workers for Christ.'

For all its unacceptable racism and imperialism this (exclusively Protestant) book contains a lasting challenge to feminists still addressed by the inhuman fettering of women in each generation and on every continent. Includes Mrs Moffat (South Africa), Mrs Gobat (Jerusalem), Mrs Mullens (Calcutta), Mrs Judson (Burma), Miss Fiske (Persia), Mrs Chalmers (New Guinea), Miss Higgins (Japan), Mrs Kilham (Sierra Leone), Mrs Wilson (Bombay), Miss Campbell (China) Mrs Kruse (Egypt), i.a. Gives some sources. Itself an important, underused source.

210 Darton, John Maw. *Heroism of Christian Women of our own time – what they have Done and are Doing, embracing their Early Training and Inner Life.*

W. Swan, Sonenschein and Allen, London. With portraits.

Preface: 'Christianity with these women is more a daily practice than a lifeless theory. ... They are inspired with a moral courage to set aside all worldly considerations for the social and religious good of the whole human race.' Includes Agnes Jones, pioneer workhouse nurse, Lady Hope, Frances Havergal and the Quaker Mrs Bright Lucas, Mary Carpenter, several missionary women (e.g. Mrs Ranyard and Anna Mackenzie), the bereaved mother Catherine Tait and the cholera nurse 'Sister Dora' – but no Josephine Butler.

211 Charles, Elizabeth. *Sketches of the Women of Christendom.*

Dedicated to the Women of India.

SPCK, London, under direction of the Tract Committee.

Preface: 'Undertaken at the request of a member of the Cambridge University Mission at Delhi, with the hope of giving our fellow-subjects, the women of India, some conception of what Christianity has done for the women of Christendom.'

Includes, after New Testament women, the martyrs Blandina, Perpetua and Felicitas, Monica, Abbess Hilda, Joan of Arc, Lady Rachel Russell, Susanna Wesley, Catherine Tait, Hannah More, Sarah Martin and Elizabeth Fry.

1881

212 Cook, Edward Dutton. *Hours with the Players.*

Chatto and Windus, London. 2 volumes.

Includes: Peg Woffington, 'Perdita' Robinson, Mrs Baddeley, Miss Smithson, Charlotte Cushman, Mrs Glover and Rachel Felix.

213 Anon. *Earnest Lives – Biographies of remarkable men and women.*

Includes: Lucy Hutchinson, Lady Rachel Russell and autodidact Scot Janet Hamilton.

1882

214 Hack, Mary Prior. *Self-Surrender* or *Consecrated Women.*

Hodder and Stoughton, London.

Introduction: 'Each sainted woman leaves her own special example for our instruction, but we are not called to blind imitation of any earthly pattern.' Includes Anne Askew, Isabel Brown, Helen Herschell (Hebrew linguist and wife of Jewish Christian minister), and Agnes Jones, i.a.

1883

215 Adams, W. H. D. *Child-life and Girlhood of Remarkable Women.*

W. Swan, Sonnenschein and Co., London.

An unchronological collection of anecdotes on every woman who occurs to him, jumping from nineteenth-century 'women of letters' to Lady Jane Grey or Joan of Arc, and ending with Mme Roland and Mme Michelet.

216 Paul, Charles Kegan. *Biographical Sketches.*

Kegan Paul and Co., London.

Notable for first inclusion of George Eliot. Deliberately vague about her 'deep religious troubles' but sympathetic about the 'special circumstances' of her inability to marry Lewes.

217 Robertson, Eric. *English Poetesses – a series of critical biographies, with illustrative extracts.*

Cassell and Co., London.

An attempt at inclusive coverage that juxtaposes the most powerful writers with the most understandably forgotten, e.g. Emily Brontë with Menella Bute Smedley. Domestic ideology: 'children are the best poems Providence meant women to produce.' Includes Aphra Behn, Duchess of Newcastle, Mrs Barbauld, Mary Lamb, Scottish poetesses, Mrs Hemans, L. E. L., Sara Coleridge, Elizabeth Barrett Browning, Christina Rossetti, Augusta Webster, Alice Meynell and Mathilde Blind, i.a.

218 Hack, Mary Prior. *Christian Womanhood.*

Hodder and Stoughton, London.

Comparatively unknown lives: Mary Fletcher, Mary Hall, Mary Boyles Brown, Elizabeth last Duchess of Gordon, Harriet Perfect, Mary Ker, Mary Calvert, Anna Backhouse and Frances Ridley Havergal.

219 Doran, John. *Their Majesties' Servants – Annals of the English Stage from Thos. Betterton to Edmund Kean.*

John C. Nimmo, London. 3 volumes. Illustrated.

Self-explanatory. Some actresses included.

219a Chapman, W. *Notable Women of the Puritan Times.*

W. Swan, Sonnenschein, London. Illustrated.

Self-explanatory. Includes both American and English women. See also the same author's work published in the same year on Scottish women – *Notable Women of the Covenant.*

1884

220 Anon. *Great Englishwomen.*

Bell's reading book for young children.

After mediaeval queens, the nine women it was thought essential for children to know were Margaret Roper, Lady Jane Grey, Lady Rachel Russell, Angelica Kauffmann, Hannah More, Elizabeth Fry, Mary Somerville ('a woman in advance of her times'), Elizabeth Barrett Browning and Florence Nightingale – all of them women of exceptional force of character and power of mind.

Interesting to compare with Anon. shilling book from Ward Lock the previous year for grown-ups, *Notable Women of our own Times*, which praised Florence Nightingale, Rosa Bonheur, Burdett-Coutts, George, Sand, Clara Schumann and Mary Carpenter.

221 Adams, W. H. D. *Celebrated Women Travellers of the 19thC.*

W. Swan, Sonnenschein, London. 8th edition 1903.

Includes: Frederika Bremer, Alexandrina Tinne, Ida Pfeiffer, Lady

Hester Stanhope, Lady Brassey, Lady Morgan, Mrs Trollope, Harriet Martineau, Isabella Bird, Lady Florence Dixie (Patagonia), Mrs Gordon-Cumming and Lady Barker (New Zealand).

222   *Adams, W. H. D. *Celebrated Women of the Victorian Period.*

F. V. White and Co., London. 2 volumes.

Intended for those readers who 'wish to know something of the life, character, and work of women whose names have become familiar as household words'. Hopes book will contribute to movement for equality of women. George Eliot (called 'Miss Evans') now included, cited as clinching evidence that 'the intellectual development of woman is, so far as England is concerned, one of the "great facts" of the nineteenth century.' Also includes Mary Somerville, Sara Coleridge, Mary Carpenter, Adelaide Procter, Jane Welsh Carlyle, Queen Victoria, Harriet Martineau, Charlotte Brontë and Mary Russell Mitford.

223   *Stowe, Harriet Beecher (ed.). *Our Famous Women.* [American.]

Unapologetic heroinism. Essays affirming the work of L. M. Alcott, Susan Anthony, Clara Barton, the Doctors Blackwell, Charlotte Cushman, Lydia Maria Child, Margaret Fuller, Julia Ward Howe, Mary Livermore, Lucretia Mott, Elizabeth Cady Stanton, Frances Willard and Harriet Beecher Stowe herself, i.a., written by their fellow feminists and Abolitionists.

224   Hack, Mary Prior. *Consecrated Women.*

Hodder and Stoughton, London.

Pious tributes to Catharine of Siena, Susanna Wesley, A. Sieveking, Charlotte Elizabeth Tonna, Margaret Wilson, Fidelia Fiske and Lena Huber.

1885

225   Hack, Mary Prior. *Faithful Service – Sketches of Christian Women.*

Hodder and Stoughton, London.

Introduction: 'There is in many minds an erroneous impression that deep spirituality and devotion to secular service are incompatible.'

Includes Methodist convert Lady Maxwell, the missionary in Burma Sarah Judson, together with the anti-slavery activist Priscilla Johnston, née Buxton, i.a.

34. The feminist journalist
Frances Power Cobbe,
from her *Life*, 1902.

226 *Hays, Frances. *Women of the Day – A Biographical Dictionary of Notable Contemporaries [of all lands]*.

Chatto and Windus, London.

Includes Louisa Alcott, Helen Allingham, Elizabeth Garrett Anderson, Mrs Bancroft, Lady Barker, Mme Belloc (née Bessie Parkes), Mme Blavatsky, Mme Bodichon, Rosa Bonheur, Emilia Boucherett, Rhoda Broughton, Frances Hodgson Burnett, Baroness Burdett-Coutts, Miss Buss, Elizabeth Charles, Eleanor Clayton, Frances Power Cobbe, Isa Craig, Emily Faithfull, Millicent Fawcett, Fanny Lewald, Florence Fenwick Miller, Mrs Molesworth, Dinah Mulock, Florence Nightingale, Margaret Oliphant, Violet Paget, Mrs Mark Pattison, Christina Rossetti, Emily Anne Shirreff, Agnes Smith, Harriet Beecher Stowe, Helen Taylor, Anne Thackeray, Pauline Viardot, Augusta Webster, Lady Wilde, and Frances Willard i.a.

Fascinating and underused source, including many nineteenth-century feminists.

227 *Higgins, Mrs Napier. *Women of Europe in the 15th and 16th Centuries*.

Hurst and Blackett, London. 2 volumes.

Based on Latin, German and French primary sources. Preface: 'The present work is an attempt to fill a void. ... Although women form one half of the human race, they are all but ignored in general history; too often only a King's mistress is allowed entry which tends to a low and unjust estimate of women. ... These vols are intended rather as a fragment of the history of woman, than as memoirs of certain gifted women ... a history of great ladies is not a history of women.' Includes Margaret of Denmark, d. 1412, Abbess Elizabeth of Holstein, early Queens of Scandinavia and of Poland and Agnes Bernauer, murdered in 1435.

228 Gillow, J. *Literary and Biographical Dictionary of English and Scots Catholics. – A Literary and biographical history or Bibliographical Dictionary of the English Catholics; from the breach with Rome in 1534 to the present time.*

Burns and Oates, London. 5 volumes.

Called 'the first book in any library of Catholic history'. Overwhelmingly male. Includes the martyr Margaret Clitherow, but not Mary Ward.

229 Banfield, F. *Biographies of Celebrities for the People.*

J. and R. Maxwell, London.

Section 8: *Eminent [Contemporary] Women*: Sarah Bernhardt, Mme Blavatsky, Mary Elizabeth Braddon, Rhoda Broughton, Baroness Burdett-Coutts, Lady Elizabeth Butler, Mrs Charlesworth, Frances Power Cobbe, Empress Eugenie, Millicent Fawcett, Elizabeth Garrett Anderson, Mrs Gladstone, Mrs Craik, Florence Nightingale, Margaret Oliphant, Ouida, Patti, Harriet Beecher Stowe, Ellen Terry and Mrs Henry Wood.

230 Stephen, Leslie (ed.). *Dictionary of National Biography. Vol. I Abbadie – Anne.*

Smith and Elder, London.

The summation of received wisdom on British collective biography, including that of women, by the end of the nineteenth century. 'Anyone interested in women's history might take the *DNB* as a starting point.' (Gillian Fenwick, *Women and the DNB ... 1885 – 1985 and Missing Persons*, Scolar Press, 1995, Introduction.)

Includes: Maria Abdy, Frances Abington, Christian Henrietta Acland, Eliza Acton, Jean Adam, Laura Addison, Adela, Queen Adelaide, Adeliza, Adeliza of Louvain, Queen Aelfgifu, Queen Aelfthryth I, and II, Grace Aguilar, Mary Aikenhead, Lucy Aikin,

Louisa Albany, Emma Albertazzi, Aldgyth, Helen Alexander, Princess Alice Maud, Princess Amelia, Lucy Anderson, Angharad the Nun, Anne, Queen of Richard II, Queen Anne, Anne of Bohemia, Anne Boleyn, Anne de Bourbon, Anne of Cleves, Anne of Denmark and Anne of Silesia.

231 Stephen, Leslie (ed.). *Dictionary of National Biography. Vol. II Annesley – Baird.*

Smith and Elder, London.

Includes: Elizabeth of Anspach, Arabella Stuart, Frances d'Arblay (Fanny Burney), Mary Armine, Cecilia Arne, Blanche Arundell, Mary Arundell, Anne Askew, Mary Astell, Princess Augusta Sophia, Sarah Aust, Jane Austen, Sarah Austin, Dr Matilda Ayrton, Sarah Bache, Ann Lady Bacon, Sophia Baddeley, Lady Grizel Baillie, Joanna Baillie and Marianne Baillie.

232 Stephen, Leslie (ed.). *Dictionary of National Biography. Vol. III Baker – Beadon.*

Smith and Elder, London.

Includes: Anne Baker, Clara Balfour, Frances Ball, Hannah Ball, Lady Mary Bankes, Sarah Banks, Anne Bannerman, Mrs Barbauld, Mary Barber, Anne Barnard, Charlotte Barnard, Mrs Barry, Elizabeth Barry, Sarah Bartley, Ann Bartholomew, Elizabeth Barton, Louisa Barwell, Sarah Bates, Lucy Bather, Queen Bathilda and Ann Baynard.

233 Stephen, Leslie (ed.). *Dictionary of National Biography. Vol. IV Beal – Biber.*

Smith and Elder, London.

Includes: Mary Beale, Lady Diana Beauclerk, Margaret Beaufort, Lady Eliza Becher, St Bega, St Begha, Aphra Behn, Lady Maria Bell, George Anne Bellamy, Bridget Bendish, Elizabeth Benger, Agnes Bennett, Mary Benwell, Queen Berengaria, Eliza Berkeley, Juliana Berners, Mary Berry, Queen Bertha, Lady Catharine Bertie (née Willoughby, Duchess of Suffolk), Matilda Betham and Jane Bewick.

1886

234 Jex-Blake, Sophia. *Medical Women.*

Oliphant, Anderson and Ferier, Edinburgh; Hamilton, Adams and Ferrier, London.

Anecdotal, unstructured history of the professional medical education of women, including midwives, in Europe since the fifteenth century and in Britain since 1871. Includes much autobiographical material as well as reference to Drs Elizabeth Blackwell, Elizabeth Garrett Anderson, Mary Scharlieb, Mary Pailthorpe, Agnes M'Laren, Edith Peachey, Ann Clark and others of the 50 women doctors registered in Britain in 1886.

235   MacSorley, Catherine. *A Few good Women and what they teach us – a Book for Girls.*

J. Hogg, London.

Religious with feminist undertones. Includes Augustine's mother Monica exemplifying Patience, Margaret Godolphin Steadfastness, Princesse de Lamballe Loyalty till Death, Mary Somerville Perseverance and Agnes Jones Thoroughness. Some fine portraits, and sources are cited.

236   Walford, Edward. *Chapters from Family Chests.*

Hurst and Blackett, London. 2 volumes.

Includes Rachel, Lady Russell, the Countess of Drogheda, the Hon. Mrs Damer ('she wanted to be buried with her tools'), Bess of Hardwick and Margaret Cavendish, Duchess of Newcastle.

237   Brown, James D. *Biographical Dictionary of Musicians.*

Alexander Gardner, London. 622 pp.

Mentions women's composing as well as performance. Includes Harriet Abrams, Mrs Crouch, Cecilia and Marianne Davies, Anne Fricker, Jenny Lind, Malibran, Mary Paton, Pasta, Mary Postans, Clara Novello, Patti, Kitty Stephens, Mme Vestris, Pauline Viardot Garcia and Clara Schumann, 'the greatest living female pianist'.

238   Stephen, Leslie (ed.). *Dictionary of National Biography. Volume V Bicheng – Bottisham.*

Smith and Elder, London.

Includes: Mrs Bicknell, Sarah Biffin, Elizabeth Billington, Margaret Bingham, Ann Bishop, Anna Blackburne, Elizabeth Blackwell, Susanna Blamire, Elizabeth Bland, Maria Bland, Mary Blandy, Marguerite Blessington, Martha Blount, Boadicea, Joan Bocher, Thomasine Bonaventure, Elizabeth Bonhote, Sarah Booth, Miss Hill Boothby and Lady Louisa Boothby.

239   Stephen, Leslie (ed.). *Dictionary of National Biography. Volume VI Bottomley – Browell.*

Smith and Elder, London.

Includes: Joan Boughton, Mrs Boutel, Catharina Bovey, Henrietta

Bowdler, Jane Bowdler, Elizabeth Bowes, Mary Bowes, Anne Bracegirdle, Ann Bradshaw, Anne Bradstreet, Barbarina Brand, Hannah Brand, Anna Bray, Charlotte Brent, Katharine Brettarg, Cecilia Brightwell, St Brigit, Frances Broderip, Anne Brontë, Charlotte Brontë, Emily Brontë, Charlotte Brooke, Lady Elizabeth and Frances Brooke.

240 Stephen, Leslie (ed.). *Dictionary of National Biography. Volume VII Brown – Burthogge.*

Smith and Elder, London.

Includes: Elizabeth Barrett Browning, Elizabeth Brownrigg, Mary Brunton, Margaret Bryan, Elspeth Buchan, Sophia Bulkeley, Agnes Bulmer, Margaret Bunn, Frances Bunsen, Mary Anne Burges, Elizabeth Burnet, Margaret Burnet, Sarah Burney and Sophia Burrell.

241 Stephen Leslie (ed.). *Dictionary of National Biography. Volume VIII Burton – Cantwell.*

Smith and Elder, London.

Includes: Catherine Burton, Lady Charlotte Bury, Elizabeth Bury, Lady Eleanor Butler, Bertha Buxton, Anne Byrne, Letitia Byrne, Jessie Cadell, Margaret Calderwood, Lady Maria Callcott, Caroline Calvert, Julia Margaret Cameron, Lucy Cameron, Anne Camm, Anna Campbell, Harriette Campbell, Willielma Campbell, Maria Campion, Ann Candler, St Cannera, Elizabeth Canning.

1887

242 Goldie, Mg. *Lives of Women Saints.*

Taken from Alban Butler (see entry 42).

243 Brooks, E. S. *Historic Girls – Stories of Girls who have influenced the History of their Time.*

G. P. Putnam's Sons, New York and London. New edition 1890.

Preface: 'Age and country, time and surroundings, make but little change in the real girl – nature, that has ever been impulsive, trusting, tender and true.' Then quotes Charles Kingsley's 'Be good, sweet maid, and let who will be clever' to neutralize the fierce heroism of girls like Yu Lin, the Empress of China, Zenobia of Almyra, Teresa of Avila and Pocohontas.

244 Coleridge, H. J. (S. J.) (ed.). *St Mary's Convent, Micklegate Bar, York.*

Burns and Oates, London.

Preface: 'A sequel to *The Life of Mary Ward* attesting to her successors' solidity, tenacity, resolution and daring and [showing that] Mary Ward left a school of souls behind as well as a great work on which they might occupy themselves. The Convent at the Bar was the only place in England where before c.1800 it was possible to educate Catholic girls. ... In the early days no-one could enter a religious house in this country or become a teacher there without incurring the most serious personal danger.' Unclear narrative line; pious praise of Mothers Winefride and Frances Bedingfield, Paston, Cornwallis, Aspinall, Clifton, Stanfield, Maxwell, Coyne, Aikenhead and Ball, i.a.

Includes Appendix naming almost all the Catholic girls educated at the Convent 1710–1886.

245   Stephen, Leslie (ed.). *Dictionary of National Biography. Volume IX Canute – Chaloner.*

Smith and Elder, London.

Includes: Maria Caradori-Allan, Lady Elizabeth Carey, Ann Cargill, Mary Carleton, Anne Carlisle, Jane Carlyle, Alice Carmylyon, Elizabeth Carne, Queens Caroline, Caroline Amelia and Caroline Matilda, Margaret Carpenter, Mary Carpenter, Elizabeth Carter, Ellen Carter, Frances Cartwright, Penelope Carwardine, Elizabeth Cary, Viscountess Falkland, Margaret Catchpole, Catherine of Valois, Catherine of Aragon, Catherine Howard, Catherine Parr, Catherine of Braganza, Ann Catley, Christiana Cavendish, Elizabeth Cavendish, Georgiana Cavendish, Margaret Cavendish Duchess of Newcastle, Princess Cecilia, Dorothea Celesia, Madame Celeste and Susannah Centilevre.

246   Stephen, Leslie (ed.). *Dictionary of National Biography. Volume X Chamber – Clarkson.*

Smith and Elder, London.

Includes Johanna Chandler, Mary Chandler, Mary Chapman, Hester Chapone, Charlotte Charke, Maria Charlesworth, Princess Charlotte Augusta, Princess Charlotte Matilda, Queen Charlotte Sophia, Lady Henrietta Chatterton, Jane Chessar, Lady Jane Cheyne, Caroline Chisholm, Lady Mary Cholmondeley, Christina of Romsey, Elizabeth Chudleigh, Lady Mary Chudleigh, Arabella Churchill, Sarah Churchill, Susannah Cibber, Claire Clairmont, Lady Elizabeth de Clare and Mary Anne Clarke.

247   Stephen, Leslie (ed.). *Dictionary of National Biography. Volume XI Clater – Condell.*

Smith and Elder, London.

Includes: Elizabeth (Cromwell) Claypole, Margaret Clement, Lady Anne Clifford, Lady Margaret Clifford, Rosamond Clifford, Margaret Clitherow, Caroline Clive, Kitty Clive, Elizabeth Cobbold, Alicia Cockburn, Catharine Cockburn, Sara Coleridge, Catherine Collignon, Mary Collyer, Lady Janet Colquhoun and Lady Elizabeth Colville.

248 Stephen, Leslie (ed.). *Dictionary of National Biography. Volume XII Condell – Craigie.*

Includes Lady Anne Conway, Elizabeth Cooper, Fanny Corbaux, Theresa Cornelys, Caroline Cornwallis, Louisa Costello, Maria Cosway, Lady Anne Coventry (d. 1763), Lady Anne Coventry (d. 1788), Maria Countess of Coventry, Hannah Cowley and Lady Mary Cowper.

1888

249 Ramsay, John of Ochtertyre. *Scotland and Scotsmen in the 18thC.*

William Blackwood and Sons, Edinburgh and London. 2 volumes.

Compiled from ten mss. volumes written 1775–1811 and edited by Alexander Allardyce.

Volume II, Chapter 9: 'Some Scottish Ladies' – Lady Hamilton of Rosehall, Lady Sarah Bruce and Lady Rachel Drummond.

250 Sadlier, Anna. *Women of Catholicity.*

Preface by author's mother: 'In contradistinction to Julia Kavanagh's *Women of Christianity* (1852) wherein professors of all forms of religious belief – from St Teresa to Elizabeth Fry ... are made to figure on the same stage, placed, as it would almost seem, on the same plane of moral excellence – my daughter desired to confine her selection of subjects to the children of the Church ... who thus made manifest ... the marvellous efficacy of her teachings in the formation of character.'

Includes fifteenth-century Irish princess Margaret O'Carroll, Isabella of Castile, Margaret Roper, Marguerite Bourgeoys, and the foundress of the Ursulines of Quebec, Marie Guyart.

251 Charles, Elizabeth. *The Martyrs and Saints of the First Twelve Centuries Studies from the lives of the Black Letter Saints of the English Calendar.*

SPCK, London. Published under the direction of the Tract Committee.

Includes Legends of the Virgin Martyrs, Saints Perpetua, Caecilia, Agnes, Agatha, Lucy, Prisca, Faith, Margaret, Catharine, Etheldreda and Audrey.

252 Marston, J. W. *Our Recent Actors – recollections of late distinguished performers of both sexes.*

Sampson Low and Co., London.

Includes Mrs Kean, Mrs Glover, Mrs Warner, Charlotte Cushman, Mme Vestris, Mrs Nisbett, Miss Nielsen, Mlle Rachel and Helen Faucit.

253 *Ross, Janet. *Three Generations of Englishwomen.*

John Murray, London. New revised edition T. Fisher Unwin, 1892.

Memoirs by their descendant of Mrs John Taylor of Norwich, Mrs Sarah Austin, translator, and Lucie Duff Gordon. Read by the young Virginia Stephen.

254 *Ewart, Henry (ed.). *True and Noble Women.*

W. Isbister, London. Illustrated.

Christian feminist. Includes: Elizabeth Fry by Francis Faithfull, Caroline Chisholm by Thos. Stephenson, Sarah Martin by H. Ewart, Mrs Carlyle by Alex Japp, 'Sister Dora' by Mrs Charles Garnett, and, notably, Mary Carpenter by Rosamond Davenport Hill.

255 Champlin, J. D. *Painters and Paintings.*

Bernard Quaritch, New York and London. 4 volumes.

35. The social reformer and child rescuer Mary Carpenter, from Ewart's *True and Noble Women*, 1888.

Includes: Sofonisba Anguiscola, Mary Beale, Rosa Bonheur, Henrietta Brouhn, Rosalba Carriera, Lavinia Fontana, Artemisia Gentileschi, Angelica Kauffmann, Elisabeth Le Brun and Maria Sybilla Merian. Gives sources for each. Favours genre painting. No Impressionists.

256 Champlin, J. D. *Music and Musicians.*

Scribners, New York. 3 volumes.

Encyclopedic short entries, mostly male, including contemporaries.

257 Cochrane, Robert. *Lives of Good and Great Women.*

W. R. Chambers, Edinburgh and London.

Besides Queen Victoria, includes Angela Burdett-Coutts, Rosa Bonheur, Octavia Hill, Eliza Fletcher, Jean Ingelow, and a substantial essay on Harriet Beecher Stowe.

258 Strickland, Agnes and Elizabeth. *Lives of the Tudor and Stuart Princesses.* F. Bell and Sons, London. Revised edition.

259 Walford, L. B. *Four Biographies from 'Blackwood': Mrs Jane Taylor, Hannah More, Elizabeth Fry, Mary Somerville.*

Blackwood and Sons, Edinburgh and London.

260 Stephen, Leslie (ed.). *Dictionary of National Biography. Volume XIII Craik – Damer.*

Smith and Elder, London.

Includes: Lady Victoire Crampton, Lucy Crane, Louisa Craven, Elizabeth Creed, Madam Cresswell, Jane Crewdson, Frances Crewe, Elizabeth Crofts, Mary Ann Cross (i.e. George Eliot), Anna Maria Crouch, Catherine Crowe, Frances Currer, St Cuthburga and Anne Damer.

262 Stephen, Leslie (ed.). *Dictionary of National Biography. Volume XIV Damon – D'Eyncourt.*

Smith and Elder, London.

Includes: Grace Darling, St Darlugdach, Frances Darusmont, Mary Davenport, Harriet Davidson, Catherine Davies, Cecilia Davies, Christian Davies, Eleanor Davies, Lucy Davies, Marianne Davies, Mary Davis, Maria Davison, Lady Jane Davy, Sophia Dawes (or Daw), Nancy Dawson and Mary Delany.

262 Stephen, Leslie (ed.). *Dictionary of National Biography. Volume XV Diamond – Drake.*

Smith and Elder, London.

Includes: Lady Anne Dick, Maria Dickons, Elizabeth Dickson, Lady Lettice Digby, Susannah Dobson, Jane Dormer, Catherine Dorset, Lady Jane Douglas, Lady Margaret Douglas and Anne Dowriche.

263 Stephen, Leslie (ed.). *Dictionary of National Biography. Volume XVI Drant – Eridge.*

Smith and Elder, London.

Includes: Annabella Drummond, Margaret Drummond, Lady Dorothea Du Bois, Lady Jane Dudley (i.e. Lady Jane Grey), Agnes Dunbar, Susanna Duncombe, Frances Dunlop, Sophia Dussek, St Dympna, St Eadburga, Queen Eadburga, Queen Eanflaed, St Ebba, Abbess Ebba, Mary Ebsworth, Emily Eden, Maria Edgeworth, St Edith and Queen Edith.

1889

264 *Pitman, Mrs E. R. *Lady Missionaries in Foreign Lands.*

Pickering and Inglis, London and Glasgow. Illustrated.

One of a series of 'Bright Biographies – stirring life stories of Christian men and women.'

36. Frontispiece to Pitman's *Lady Missionaries in Foreign Lands*, 1889.

Preface: 'Almost invariably, male missionaries are denied access to native women ... especially in India and all Eastern countries. ... Therefore [the] work of teaching *Heathen Women* to come to Jesus belongs emphatically to *Christian Women*. It is only in Christian lands that women occupy their proper place. In all other countries they are drudges, slaves, or victims; but equals or companions, *never!* ... Woman is above man in her sentimental, emotional, and religious nature.' Includes Ann Judson (Burmah), Mrs Johnston (West Indies), Mrs Gobat (Abyssinia), Mrs Wilkinson (Zululand), Mrs Cargill (Friendly Islands). A fascinating underused source.

265 Keeling, Annie. *Eminent Methodist Women.*

Charles H. Kelly, London. 2nd edition 1893.

Treats all the women as holy saints. Includes Susanna Wesley, Mary Bosanquet, Lady Mary Fitzgerald, Elizabeth Mortimer, Barbara Heck, Caroline Walker, Jane Tucker and Anne Lutton.

266 *Wheeler, J. M. *Biographical Dictionary of Freethinkers of all ages and nations.*

The Pioneer Press, London.

Overwhelmingly male but does include Marie Anderson, Susan Anthony, Annie Besant, Eliza Sharples Carlile, Jane Carlile, Mme de Chatelet, Lydia Maria Child, Lucy Colman, Sophie de Condorcet, Maria Deraismes, Mme Du Deffand, George Eliot, Margaret Fuller, Matilda Gage (who 'with Susan Anthony and Elizabeth Stanton considers the Church the great obstacle to woman's progress'), Hypatia, Harriet Law, Emma Martin, Harriet Martineau, Lucretia Mott, 'Ouida', Violet Paget ('Vernon Lee'), Olga Plumacher, Amy Post, Matilda Roalfe, Mme Roland, Ernestine Rose, George Sand, Olive Schreiner, Edith Simcox, Bertha von Suttner, Mrs Humphrey Ward, Mary Wollstonecraft, Frances Wright and Helen Zimmern.

No Eleanor Marx or Harriet Taylor Mill, but a valuable underused source for women's history.

267 Fittis, Robert Scott. *Heroines of Scotland.*

Alexander Gardner, London.

Includes Isobel, Countess of Buchan, 'Black Agnes' of Dunbar, Margaret Keith, Janet Douglas, the Ladies Ogilvie and Lady Sophia Lindsay, i.a.

268 Buffen, F. F. *Musical Celebrities.*

Chapman & Hall, London.

37. The suffragist leader
Millicent Fawcett.

Brief professional biographies of Adelina Patti, Jeanne Douste and
Marcella Sembrich, i.a. Fine photos.

269   *Fawcett, Mrs Henry. *Some Eminent Women of Our Times*.

Macmillan and Co., London and Edinburgh.

Sketches originally 'intended chiefly for working women and young
people' and published in *The Mothers' Companion*. Secular feminism.
It 'was hoped it would be an encouragement to ... be reminded how
much good work had been done in various ways by women'. Includes
Elizabeth Fry, Mary Carpenter, Caroline Herschel, Mary Somerville,
Harriet Martineau, Florence Nightingale, Agnes Jones, the Brontës,
E. B. Browning, Jane Austen, Dorothy Wordsworth, 'Sister Dora'
and the American Abolitionists Prudence Crandall and Lucretia
Mott. Exudes a palpable, exhilarating joy at women's recent
achievements for humanity.

270   Stephen, Leslie (ed.). *Dictionary of National Biography. Volume XVII
Edward – Erskin*.

Smith and Elder, London.

Includes: Elizabeth Edwin, Sarah Egerton, Queen Eleanor, Eleanor
of Castile, Eleanor of Provence, Elisabeth of Hungary, Elizabeth
Queen of Edward IV, Elizabeth Queen of Henry VII, Elizabeth I,
Elizabeth of Austria, Abbess Elizabeth of Holstein, Princess

Elizabeth of the Palatinate, Elizabeth of Russia, Princess Elizabeth Stuart, Jane Elliot, Charlotte Elliott, Grace Elliott, Sarah Stickney Ellis, Hester Elphinstone, Margaret Elphinstone, Elizabeth Elstob, Queen Emma and Francesca Epine.

271 Stephen, Leslie (ed.). *Dictionary of National Biography. Volume XVIII Esdaile – Finan.*

Includes: Saint Ethelburga, Saint (and Queen) Etheldreda, Ethelfleda, Juliana Ewing, Priscilla Fane, Lady Anne Fanshawe, Catherine Fanshawe, Elizabeth Farren, Ellen Farren, Margaret Fell, Elizabeth Fenning, Lavinia Fenton, Henrietta Fermor, Susan Ferrier, Sarah Fielding and Anne Fiennes.

272 Stephen, Leslie (ed.). *Dictionary of National Biography. Volume XIX Finch – Forman.*

Smith and Elder, London.

Includes: Anne Finch Countess of Winchilsea, Catherine Fisher, Mary Fisher, Mary Fitton, Lady Elizabeth Fitzgerald, Lady Katherine Fitzgerald, Lady Pamela Fitzgerald, Mrs Fitzhenry, Mrs Fitzherbert, Mary Fitzroy, Fanny Fitzwilliam, Mary Ann Flaxman, Miss Fleming, Marjory Fleming, Eliza Fletcher, Eliza Flower, Lucretia Folkes, Ruth Follows and Maria Foote.

273 Stephen, Leslie (ed.). *Dictionary of National Biography. Volume XX Forrest – Garner.*

Smith and Elder, London.

Includes: Caroline Fox, Elizabeth Fox, Mary Frampton, Anne Francis, Jocosa Frankland, Eleanor Franklin, Lady Jane Franklin, St Frideswitha, Mary Frith ('Moll Cut-purse'), Elizabeth Fry, Lady Georgiana Fullerton, Mary Gabriel and Mrs Gardner.

1890

274 Thistelton-Dyer, T. F. *The Loves and Marriages of some Eminent Persons.*

Ward and Downey, London. 2 volumes.

Gossip concerning 'eccentric marriages', e.g. Anna Jameson's; 'irregular marriages', e.g. Mrs Chudleigh's; 'unhappy marriages', e.g. Mrs Hemans', Mrs Inchbald's, L. E. L.'s and Charlotte Smith's; and 'marriage by consent', e.g. George Eliot's and G. H. Lewes'.

275 Stephen, Leslie and Lee, Sidney, (eds). *Dictionary of National Biography. Volume XXI Garnett – Gloucester.*

Smith and Elder, London.

Includes: Elizabeth Gaskell, Margaret Gatty, Elizabeth Gaunt, Jenny Geddes, Artemisia Gentileschi, Lady Elizabeth Germain, Lady Grace Gethin, Mrs Gibbs, Susan Gibson, Ann Gilbert, Elizabeth Gilbert, Marie Dolores Gilbert (i.e. Lola Montez), Anne Gilchrist, Margaret Gillies, Mary Girling, Maria Gisborne and Hannah Glasse.

276 Stephen, Leslie and Lee, Sidney (eds). *Dictionary of National Biography. Volume XXII Glover – Graves.*

Smith and Elder, London.

Includes: Jean Glover, Julia Glover, Isabella Glyn, Lady Godiva, Margaret Godolophin, Catherine Godwin, Mary Wollstonecraft Godwin, Anna Goldsmid, Charlotte Goodall, Elizabeth Gordon, Lady Henrietta Gordon, Jane Gordon, Lucie Duff Gordon, Catherine Gore, Emily Gosse, Mary Grace, Miss Graddon, Clementina Graham, Janet Graham, Anne Grant and Elizabeth Grant.

277 Stephen, Leslie and Lee, Sidney (eds). *Dictionary of National Biography. Volume XXIII Gray – Haighton.*

Smith and Elder, London.

Includes: Maria Gray, Eliza Green, Mary Everett Green, Anne Greene, Dora Greenwell, Lady Elizabeth Grey, Constantia Grierson, Elizabeth Griffith, Ann Griffiths, Elizabeth Grimston, Harriet Grote, Lady Gundrada, Elizabeth Gunning, Susannah Gunning, Anna Gurney, Eleanor, (i.e. Nell) Gwyn and Maria Hack.

278 Stephen, Leslie and Lee, Sidney (eds). *Dictionary of National Biography. Volume XXIV Hailes – Harriott.*

Smith and Elder, London.

Includes: Lady Anne Halkett, Mrs Agnes Hall, Anna Maria Hall, Margaret Hallahan, Anne, Duchess of Hamilton, Lady Anne Hamilton, Elizabeth Hamilton de Grammont, Elizabeth Hamilton, Lady Emma Hamilton, Janet Hamilton, Lady Mary Hamilton, Mrs A. Harding, Elizabeth Hardy, Lady Brilliana Harley and Sarah Harlowe.

1891

279 *Chapman, Mrs E. F. *Sketches of some Distinguished Indian Women.*

W. H. Allen, London and Calcutta.

Preface by Marchioness of Dufferin and Alva: 'I have never read anything ... more likely to be useful to the cause of female education in India.' Introduction shows strong feminist solidarity with Indian women, especially with sonless widows. In favour of Higher Education for Indian Women, noting that they had been eligible for University Degrees before British women won that right.

Includes: Ramabai, Dr Anandibai Joshee, Toru Dutt and Cornelia Sorabji.

280 Adams, W. H. D. *Some Historic Women or Biographical Studies of Women who made History.*

J. Hogg, London. With portraits.

Twelve types of noble womanhood: Joan of Arc, Mme Roland, Catherine of Siena, Elizabeth of Hungary, Queen Christina, Louisa, Queen of Prussia, Elizabeth I, i.a. He gives his historical sources.

281 Lee, Sidney (ed.). *Dictionary of National Biography. Volume XXV Harris – Henry I.*

Smith and Elder, London.

Includes: Mary Harrison, Susannah Harrison, Elizabeth Hartley, Margaret Harvey, Isabella Harwood, Elizabeth Hasell, Lady Elizabeth Hastings, Lady Flora Hastings, Lady Selina Hastings (i.e. Countess of Huntingdon), Martha Hatfield, Frances Havergal, Susanna Hawkins, Lucy Hay, Mary Hay, Mrs Hayes, Catherine Hayes, Eliza Haywood, Mary Heaton, Felicia Hemans, Barbara Hemphill, Mary Hennell, Henrietta Duchess of Orleans and Queen Henrietta Maria.

282 Lee, Sidney (ed.). *Dictionary of National Biography. Volume XXVI Henry II – Hindley.*

Smith and Elder, London.

Includes: Lucy Herbert, Mary Herbert, Countess of Pembroke, Caroline Herschel, Lady Mary Hervey, Lady Harriet Hesketh, Phoebe Hessel, Lady Sarah Hewley, Saint Hilda and Saint Hildilid.

283 Lee, Sidney (ed.). *Dictionary of National Biography. Volume XXVII Hindmarsh – Hovenden.*

Smith and Elder, London.

Includes: Miss E. Hippisley, Jane Hippisley, Lady Elizabeth Hoby, Margaret Hodson, Barbara Hofland, Anne Holbrook, Ellen Hollond, Laura Honey, Maria Honner, Mary Honywood, Elizabeth Hooton, Anne Hope, Susannah Hopton, Susanna Hornebolt and Christiana Horton.

284 Lee, Sidney (ed.). *Dictionary of National Biography. Volume XXVIII Howard – Inglethorpe.*

Smith and Elder, London.

Includes: Elizabeth Howard, Henrietta Howard, Countess of Suffolk, Mary Howitt, Mary Hudson, Margaret Hughes, Anne Humby, Anna Hume, Lady Agnes Hungerford, Arabella Hunt, Anne Hunter, Rachel Hunter, Anne Hutchinson, Lucy Hutchinson, Catherine Hutton, Anne Hyde, Duchess of York, Catherine Hyde, Jane Hyde, Agnes Ibbetson and Elizabeth Inchbald.

1892

285 Boase, F. *Modern English Biography, containing many thousand concise memoirs of persons who have died between the years 1851–1900 with an index of the most interesting matter.*

Privately printed limited edition, Cornwall. 1892–1901. 3 volumes.

Includes many minor figures of the late nineteenth century based on newspaper obituaries, with useful sources. An underused resource for women's history.

286 *Hamilton, Catherine J. *Women Writers, Their Works and Ways.*

Ward Lock, Bowden and Co., London. 1892–3. 2 volumes.

Preface to 1st Series: 'To tell the life-stores of some famous women writers – how they attained success and how they enjoyed it is the object of these slight biographical sketches. ... It is not among writers that the happiest women are generally found. ... Happy women, whose hearts are satisfied and full, have little need of utterance. ... Many have to struggle against loneliness, poverty, depression and monotony, e.g. Caroline Norton, Charlotte Brontë, Frederika Bremer, L. E. L., Felicia Hemans.'

Volume I includes Fanny Burney, Mrs Inchbald, Mme de Stael, Mrs Barbauld, Hannah More, Lady Anne Barnard, Joanna Baillie, Lady Nairn, Mrs Radcliffe, Amelia Opie and Jane Austen ('the best storyteller of the age ... unappreciated till after her death') as well as Lady Morgan, Susan Ferrier, Mary Russell Mitford and the Countess of Blessington. No Mary Wollstonecraft.

Preface to 2nd Series: 'Our women writers have become less amusing; they are terribly in earnest, much impressed with the seriousness of life, and with difficult social problems.' Volume II includes Mrs Hemans, Mrs Jameson, Frederika Bremer, Harriet Martineau (admiring her journalism but deploring her atheism), L. E. L., Caroline Norton, Elizabeth Barrett Browning, Mrs Gaskell, Charlotte Brontë, George Eliot (explaining but not excusing the union with Lewes and regretting her atheism), Adelaide Procter and Louisa May Alcott. A lively personal response, helped by material from Miss Gaskell and Helen Blackburn.

287 O'Donoghue, David, *The Poets of Ireland, A Biographical Dictionary*.

Published by the author, London.

Host of notes on mainly minor writers. Includes Mrs C. Alexander, Mary Balfour, Mary Barber, Mary Benn, Elizabeth Boyd, Teresa Boylan, Mary Cusack (recusant nun), Maria Edgeworth, Mrs S. C. Hall, Rose Kavanagh, Lady Morgan, Fanny Parnell, Annie Paterson Dr mus., Laetitia Pilkington, Dora Sigerson, Mary Tighe, Charlotte Tonna, and Lady Wilde, i.a.

288 Lee, Sidney (ed.). *Dictionary of National Biography. Volume XXIX Inglis – John*.

Smith and Elder, London.

Includes: Margaret Inglis, Elizabeth Inverarity, Empress Isabella, Princess Isabella, Queen Isabella, d. 1358, Eleanor James, Anna Jameson, Queen Jane of Scotland, Queen Jane Seymour, Frances Jarman (i.e. Ellen Ternan), Ann Jebb, Henrietta Jenkin, Mary Jevons, Geraldine Jewsbury, Maria Jewsbury, Joan of Arc, Joan, Queen of Scotland, d. 1238, Joan, Queen of Scotland, d. 1362, Joan, Queen of Sicily, Joan (the Fair Maid of Kent) and Elizabeth Jocelin.

289 Lee, Sidney (ed.). *Dictionary of National Biography. Volume XXX Johnes – Kenneth*.

Smith and Elder, London.

Includes: Esther Johnson ('Vanessa'), Christian Johnstone, Avonia Jones, Charlotte Jones, Dorothy Jordan, Julian of Norwich, Angelica Kauffmann, Julia Kavanagh, Ellen Kean, Annie Keary, Hester Kello, Frances Kelly, Mary Kelty, Adelaide Kemble, Elizabeth Kemble, Maria Kemble, Priscilla Kemble, Margery Kempe, Emma Kendrick, Mrs Kennedy and Grace Kennedy.

290 Lee, Sidney (ed.). *Dictionary of National Biography. Volume XXXI Kennett – Lambart*.

Smith and Elder, London.

Includes: Victoria, Duchess of Kent, Louise de Keroualle, Dame Alice Kettle (or Kyteler), Lady Mary Keys, Hannah Kilham, Anne Killigrew, Lady Katherine Killigrew, Jean Kincaid, Frances King, Anna Kingsford, Lady Mary Jane Kinnaird, Elizabeth Kirby, Lady Catherine Kirkhoven, Ellis Cornelia Knight, Lady Henrietta Knight, Mary Knight, Mrs Knipp (or Knep), Mary Knowles, Frances Lacy, Harriette Lacy, Lady Caroline Lamb and Mary Lamb.

291 Lee, Sidney (ed.). *Dictionary of National Biography. Volume XXXII Lambe – Leigh*.

Smith and Elder, London.

Includes: Laetitia Landon, Jessica Landseer, Jane Lane, Mary Latter, Mary Lawrance, Jane Lead, Mary Leadbeater, Caroline Leakey, Mary Leapor, Anna Le Breton, Ann Lee, Harriet Lee, Rachel Lee, Sarah Lee, Sophia Lee, Mrs Alicia Le Fanu, Miss Alicia Le Fanu and Lettice, Countess of Leicester.

292 Pitman, Mrs E. R. *Lady Hymn Writers.*

T. Nelson and Sons, London.

Preface: 'It takes poetic feeling, fervent devotion, and religious experience to make a good hymn.'

Chapter 1:

> In singing hymns, the Church militant forgets to quarrel; and so our hymn books bear musical and eloquent witness to the inward unity of our faith. In this one form of service there is neither Catholic nor Protestant ... for all alike praise God, and are 'one in Him'.

An encyclopaedic overview, including Frances Havergal, Mrs Barbauld, Adelaide Procter, Helen Maria Williams, the Brontës, Mary Howitt, Dora Greenwell, Christina Rossetti, Jane Taylor, Mrs Alexander and the Indian Ellen Lakshmi Goreh. An underused source.

1893

293 *Pitman, Mrs E. R. *Missionary Heroines in Eastern Lands: Woman's Work in Mission Fields.*

S. W. Partridge, London. Illustrated.

Preface: 'The annals of Christian Missions furnish copious records of womanly heroism. From the days of Ann H. Judson, in the early part of this century, until now, the succession has not failed. ... As we think of reward, we turn to the days of Christ upon earth, when He told His disciples that, as they had followed Him through contumely and hatred, and kingly persecution, so great should be their reward in heaven.'

Includes Mrs Alexina Mackay Ruthquist, 1848–1892, Presbyterian missionary in the Hindu Zenanas in Nagpoor and among the Gond hill tribes; Mrs Bowen Thompson, founder of girls' schools in Syria in the 1860s; Dr Mary McGeorge, medical missionary in Ahmedabad until 1891; and Mary Louisa Whately, founder of schools in Cairo, 1860–1889. 'Miss Whately was always most interested in the condition of the women of Egypt.'

294 Crosland, Mrs Newton. *Landmarks of a Literary Life, 1820 – 1892.*

Sampson Low, London.

38. The missionary and girls' educationalist in Egypt, Mary Louisa Whately, from Pitman's *Missionary Heroines in Eastern Lands*, 1893.

Anecdotes of the Howitts, Mrs Loudon, Rosa Bonheur, Mrs S. C. Hall, Margaret Fuller, Harriet Beecher Stowe, Geraldine Jewsbury, Elizabeth Barrett Browning.

295　Anon. *Eminent Persons: The Times Obituaries.*

7 volumes. Only two women judged worthy of inclusion, Harriet Martineau and George Eliot in Volume II.

296　Smith, G. Barnett. *Women of Renown – Nineteenth Century Studies.*

W. H. Allen, London.

Preface: 'I have endeavoured to make these studies of eminent women of the 19thC. as representative as possible. The fields covered embrace the literary, the scientific, the musical, the dramatic, the philanthropic and the adventurous.'

Includes Frederika Bremer, Marguerite Countess of Blessington, George Eliot, Jenny Lind, Mary Somerville, George Sand, Mary Carpenter, Sydney Lady Morgan, Rachel (Mme Felix), Lady Hester Stanhope. Omits Jane Austen, Charlotte Brontë and Mrs Browning because he had written about them before in the *Cornhill*, republished in his *Poets and Novelists.*

297　Walford, L. B. *Twelve English Authoresses.*

Longmans Green, London.

A woman critic writes sympathetically about Hannah More, Fanny

Burney, Maria Edgeworth, Harriet Martineau, Jane Austen, Felicia Hemans, Mary Somerville, Jane Taylor, Charlotte Brontë, Elizabeth Gaskell, E. B. Browning and George Eliot.

298 Dowie, Muriel Menie (ed.). *Women Adventurers.*

T. Fisher Unwin, London. Volume 15 of 19 volume series.

Reprints original documents recounting the lives of Mme Velazquez, Hannah Snell, Mary Anne Talbot and Christian Davies. Introduction mentions eighteenth-century women pirates Mary Read and Anne Bonney who may be read about in Charles Johnson, *A general History of the Robberies and Murders of the Most Notorious Pyrates* (1724), later ascribed to Defoe, and in Charles Ellms, *The Pirates Own Book or Authentic Narratives of the Lives, Exploits and Executions of the Most Celebrated Sea Robbers* (1837, 1844).

299 *Blackburn, Helen. *Collection of portraits of eminent British women as exhibited at Chicago in 1893.*

Women's Printing Society Ltd, London.

Mounted by a leading British Suffragist and biographer of Lydia Becker for the International Exhibition in Chicago and then presented to the Women's Hall of the University of Bristol in 1894.

> They do far more than clothe the walls ... they ... remind us of the noble philanthropic women who have given their lives to lighten others' burdens ... of the many modern authoresses who have given so much time and thought to the writing of ... novels. Especially does the group over the mantelpiece appeal to the student and call forth her admiration for it contains the portraits of the Pioneers in the Education of Women, and to these, more than to any others, do the girls of to-day owe a debt of loving gratitude, for it is they who fought for a woman's right to be well-educated, and who won the battle for her. This unique collection – the pride of our Reading Room – also comprises photographs of many highly-gifted women, who by their dramatic or poetical genius, and their skill in painting or in music have provided us with some of the best material for artistic culture.
>
> (*The Magnet*, University of Bristol, 21 June 1900)

This collection is now lost. The annotated Catalogue is held in Girton College Library, Cambridge. The portraits are grouped under Mediaeval, Tudor, seventeenth- and eighteenth-century women; Pioneers in Philanthropy and the Advancement of Women; Pioneers in Education; Royal Ladies (contemporary); Literature, Painting, Music and Drama. In the late nineteenth century Helen Blackburn singles out Lydia Becker, Caroline Ashurst Biggs, Barbara Bodichon, Jessie Boucherett, Frances Buss, Josephine Butler, Julia Cameron, Mary Carpenter, A. J. Clough, F. P. Cobbe, Emily Davies, the

Marchioness of Dufferin and Alba, Matilda Betham-Edwards, George Eliot, Millicent Fawcett, Maria Grey, Jane Harrison, Anna Haslam, Rosamond Davenport Hill, Mrs Oliphant, Jane Nassau Senior, Emily Shirreff, Ethel Smyth, Clementina Taylor, Ellen Terry and Isabella Tod, i.a.

300 Buffen, F. F. *Musical Celebrities, Second Series.*

Chapman & Hall, London.

Includes Emma Albani, Nellie Melba, Lilian Nordica, Marie Roze, Emma Calvi, Sofia and Giulia Ravogli, Minne Hauk, Marguerite de Pachmann and many others. Fine photographs.

301 *Willard, Frances, and Livermore, Mary. *Woman of the Century.*

[American].

Illustrated by photographs. Revised edition 1897.

'Among all the cyclopaedias and books about famous women this is intended to be unique. ... The 19th century is the women's century – we believe that ... these pages will bring astonishment at the vast array of woman's achievement in hundreds of new vocations.'

39. The singer Nellie Melba, from Buffen's *Musical Celebrities*, 1893.

Includes Susan Anthony, Lucretia Mott, Lucy Stone, Mrs Cady Stanton, Louisa Alcott, Harriet Beecher Stowe, Frances Willard and Mary Livermore but no Emily Dickinson or Sara Josepha Hale and no African-Americans such as Harriet Tubman or Sojourner Truth.

302   Lee, Sidney (ed.). *Dictionary of National Biography. Volume XXXIII Leighton – Lluelyn.*

Smith and Elder, London.

Includes: Charlotte Lennox, Elizabeth Le Noir, Harriet Leveson-Gower, Amy Levy, Lady Maria Lewis, Lady Jane Lewson, Hannah Lightfoot, Jenny Lind, Maria Linley, Mary Linley, Mary Linskill, Mary Linwood, Lady Alice Lisle, Hariett Litchfield, Marie Litton and Charlotte Livingstone.

303   Lee, Sidney (ed.). *Dictionary of National Biography. Volume XXXIV Llwyd – Maccartney.*

Smith and Elder, London.

Includes: Mary Lofthouse, Amelia Long, Lady Catherine Long, Maria Longworth, Jane Loudon, Maria Lovell, Margaret Bright Lucas, Theodora Lynch, Agnes Lyon, Rosina Bulwer Lytton, Catherine Macaulay, Catherine McAuley and Margaret M'Avoy.

304   Lee, Sidney (ed.). *Dictionary of National Biography. Volume XXXV MacCarwell – Maltby.*

Smith and Elder, London.

Includes: Flora Macdonald, Mrs Macfarlane, Matilda Mackarness, Mary Mackellar, Maria Macklin, Agnes Maclehose, Mary Macleod, Martha Magee, Bathsua Makin and Sarah Malcolm.

305   Lee, Sidney (ed.). *Dictionary of National Biography. Volume XXXVI Malthus – Mason.*

Smith and Elder, London.

Includes: Richmal Mangnall, Mary de la Riviere Manley, Marie Manning, Jane Marcet, Saint Margaret, Queen of Scotland, d. 1093, Margaret, Queen of Scotland, d. 1541, Margaret of Burgundy, Margaret of Anjou, Margaret of Scotland, d. 1445, Jane Marshall, Maria Marten, Mary Martin, Sarah Martin, Harriet Martineau, Queen Mary Tudor, Princess Mary of Orange, Mary, Queen of Scots, Mary II, Mary of France, Mary of Gueldres, Mary of Guise, Mary of Modena, Princess Mary of Hesse, Princess Mary of Hanover, Lady Abigail Masham and Lady Damaris Masham.

1894

306   Johnson, Joseph. *Earnest Women: Their Efforts, Struggles, and Triumphs.*

Nelson and Sons, London.

Preface: Original title 'Willing Hearts and Ready Hands' had sold in large numbers in America and the colonies. Author hopes that its examples 'of loving and useful lives ... may be ... a stimulus and incentive to wise and truthful living and may be the means of inducing many a dear and good girl to become an earnest woman.' Quintessential 'Victorianism'. Totally unsystematic but browsing yields some surprises.

307   Mayer, Townshend Gertrude. *Women of Letters.*

Richard Bentley and Son, London. 2 volumes. Illustrated.

Preface: Author aims 'to give some idea of the lives and characters of the women themselves, mainly in their own words, supplemented by the recollections of their contemporaries.' Includes Margaret Duchess of Newcastle, Mary, Countess Cowper, Lady Hervey, Lady Mary Wortley Montagu, Mrs Delany, Elizabeth Montagu, Lady Anne Barnard, the Misses Berry, Elizabeth Inchbald, Amelia Opie, Lady Morgan, Miss Mitford, Mary Shelley and Lady Duff Gordon.

308   Adams, W. H. D. *A Book of Earnest Lives* or *Good Samaritans.*

Swan Sonnenschein, London. 7th edition. 403 pp. Illustrated.

A gender-integrated work, principally focusing on British social

40. The nurse Dorothy Wyndlow Pattison, 'Sister Dora', from Adams' *Book of Earnest Lives*, 1894.

interventionists under the headings 'Work in the educational field', 'Work on behalf of the slave,' 'Work in the mission field', 'Prison reform' and 'The poor are always with us'. Includes: Mary Wortley Montagu, Mary Carpenter, Elizabeth Fry, Amelia Sieveking, Mrs Mompesson and 'Sister Dora'. A useful condensation of only patchily acknowledged sources on modern Good Samaritans.

309   Smith, George Barnett. *Noble Womanhood.*

Society for Christian Knowledge, London. 361 pp.

Includes Harriet Beecher Stowe.

310   Lee, Sidney, (ed.). *Dictionary of National Biography. Volume XXXVII Masquerier – Millying.*

Smith and Elder, London.

Includes: Mary Masters, Louisa Mathews (Madam Vestris), Queen Matilda (d. 1083), Queen Matilda (d. 1118), Queen Matilda (d. 1152), Matilda of Saxony, Empress Matilda, Isabella Mattocks, Winifred Maxwell, Countess of Nithsdale, Elizabeth Mayo, Anne Mee, Mary Meeke, Harriot Mellon, Elizabeth Melville, Adah Menken, Eliza Meteyard, Saint Mildburga, Saint Mildred, Sibella Miles, Lady Anna Miller and Lydia Miller.

311   Lee, Sidney (ed.). *Dictionary of National Biography. Volume XXXVIII Milman - More.*

Smith and Elder, London.

Includes: Mary Russell Mitford, Modwenna, Mme Mohl, Mary Monck, Mary Monckton, Elizabeth Montagu, Lady Mary Wortley Montagu, Henrietta Montalba, Eleanor of Montfort, Susanna Moodie, Ann Moore, Gertrude More and Hannah More.

312   Lee, Sidney (ed.). *Dictionary of National Biography. Volume XXXIX Morehead – Myles.*

Smith and Elder, London.

Includes: Alice Morgan, Lady Morgan, Mrs Favell Mortimer, Mary Moser, Rosoman Mountain, Anne Mozley, Dinah Mulock (Mrs Craik), Marie Murphy, Amelia Murray, Elizabeth Murray, Mrs Elizabeth Murray, Mrs Gaston Murray, Annie and Martha Mutrie and Jane Myddleton.

313   Lee, Sidney (ed.). *Dictionary of National Biography. Volume XXXX Myllar – Nicholls.*

Smith and Elder, London.

Includes: Constance Naden, Nano Nagle, Carolina Nairne, 'Mother Needham', Lilian Neilson, Frances Nelson, Nesta and Ann Newton.

1895

314 Hemachandra, Narayara. *Noble Deeds of Women and Girls.*

Indian publication.

Not seen.

315 Telford, J. C. *Women in the Mission Field.*

C. H. Kelly, London.

Not seen.

316 Lee, Sidney (ed.). *Dictionary of National Biography. Volume XLI Nichols – O'Dugan.*

Smith and Elder, London.

Includes: Margaret Nicholson, Mrs Nicol, Emma Nicol, Louisa Nisbett, Non Fendigaid the Blessed, Marianne North, Caroline Norton, Frances Norton, Marianne Nunn, Margaret O'Carroll and Mary O'Donnell.

317 Lee, Sidney (ed.). *Dictionary of National Biography. Volume XLII O'Duinn – Owen.*

Smith and Elder, London.

Includes: Elizabeth Ogborne, Anne Oldfield, Ellen O'Leary, Emma Oliver, Martha Oliver, Grace O'Malley, Kathleen O'Meara, Amelia Opie, Mary Orger, Dorothy Osborne, Ruth Osborne, Queen Ostrith, St Osyth and Alice Owen.

318 Lee, Sidney (ed.). *Dictionary of National Biography. Volume XLIII Owens – Passelewe.*

Smith and Elder, London.

Includes: Isobel Pagan, Lady Dorothy Pakington, Fanny Palliser, Alicia Palmer, Charlotte Palmer, Lady Eleanor Palmer, Mary Palmer, Julia Pardoe, Euphrosyne Parepa-Rosa, Maria Parke, Emma Parker, Fanny Parnell, Eliza Parsons, Elizabeth Parsons (d. 1807), Elizabeth Parsons (d. 1873) and Gertrude Parsons.

319 Lee, Sidney (ed.). *Dictionary of National Biography. Volume XLIV Paston – Percy.*

Includes: Emma Paterson, Janet Patey, Mary Paton, Carlotta Patti, Dorothea Pattison ('Sister Dora'), Isabella Paul, Lucy Peacock, Cora Pearl, Margaret Pearson, Catherine Pennefeather, Elizabeth Penrose ('Mrs Markham'), Dolly Pentreath and Lady Elizabeth Percy.

1896

320 *Eckenstein, Lina. *Woman under Monasticism. Chapters on Saint-lore and Convent life between AD 500–AD 1500.*

Cambridge University Press. Reissued, 1963, by Russell and Russell, New York.

Dedicated to Karl and Maria Pearson.

A pioneering work of revisionist, rehabilitatory, feminist history, confined to English and German women. Immensely learned and wide-ranging, translating sources from mediaeval Latin, Middle High German, Anglo-Saxon, Middle English and French, as well as utilizing the most recent scholarship.

Preface:

'For women especially the convent fostered some of the best sides of intellectual, moral and emotional life. ... The woman–saint and the nun are however figures the importance of which has hitherto been little regarded. ... The saint is thrust aside as a representative of gross superstition, and the nun is looked upon as a slothful and hysterical, if not a dissolute character. [cf. Baring-Gould, entry 181] ... That these women appeared in a totally different light to their contemporaries is generally overlooked. ... In losing the possibility of religious profession at the beginning of the 16th Century, women lost the last chance that remained to them of an activity outside the home circle. ... The right to self-development and social responsibility which the woman of to-day so persistently asks for is in many ways analogous to the right which the convent secured to womankind a thousand years ago.'

Women referred to more than once include: St Aebbe [Ebba], abbess Aelflaed, abbess Aethelburg[a], St Aethelthrith, St Afra, St Agatha, St Agnes, abbess Agnes, Anne of Silesia, St Balthild, Basina, St Bridget of Sweden, Bugga, Chrodield, abbess Eadburg, St Elisabeth of Hungary, St Elis of Schonau, Elizabeth Shelley, St Genevieve of Paris, abbess Gerberg of Gandersheim, St Gertrud of Helfta, abbess Gertrud, St Godeleva, St Gunthild, St Hedwig of Silesia, St Hild[a] of Whitby, Hildegarde of Bingen, St Hildelith, Hroswith of Gandersheim, abbess Ingetrud, St Lufthildis, St and Queen Margaret of Scotland, abbess Mathilda of Quedlinburg, Mechthild, beguine, Mechthild of Helfta, St Mildthrith [Mildred], St Odilia, St Pharaildis, St Radegund, St Reinild, St Sexburga, Tecla, abbess Tetta of Wimbourne, St Ursula, St Verena, St Walburg[a] and abbess Wethburg.

321 Griffith, Frederic. *Notable Welsh Musicians of Today, with portraits, biographies, etc.*

F. Goodwen, London. 4th edition.

Principally musicians and singers, but includes two women composers, Llewela Davies and Margaret Davies.

322   *Hill, Georgiana. *Women in English Life from Mediaeval to Modern Times.*

Richard Bentley and Son, London. 2 volumes.

Not itself a work of collective biography but its social historical review is grounded in biographical evidence. Volume 2 on the eighteenth and nineteenth centuries especially informative. Includes women as travellers, explorers, musicians, composers, artists, writers, nurses, educationalists, in business, factories, domestic service, the Salvation Army and the mission field, as well as women humanitarians: Hannah More, Mrs Trimmer, Elizabeth Fry, Mary Carpenter, Harriet Martineau, Emma Cons, Josephine Butler, Louisa Twining, Frances Power Cobbe and Ellice Hopkins. Vigorously pro women's suffrage, citing Mrs John Stuart Mill, Barbara Bodichon and Lydia Becker.

A landmark work in English women's history. The author also wrote *A History of English Dress.*

323   Mundell, Frank. *Heroines of Daily Life.*

The Sunday School Union, London. Illustrated.

The author also wrote inspiriting stories for young boys about balloon adventures, stories of the fire brigade, the lifeboat, the Victoria Cross, the North Pole, etc.

Anecdotes of noteworthy deeds of self-sacrificing heroism performed by women and girls – many unnamed – on impulse in the exigencies of ordinary life. Presumably intended, as were its sequels in Mundell's 'Heroines' Library', as girls' Sunday School Prize books.

324   Mundell, Frank. *Heroines of Mercy.*

The Sunday School Union, London. Illustrated.

Focuses on 'all those who whether as nurses or philanthropists, devote their time and energy to ... the suffering, the ignorant and the poor.'

Includes Elizabeth Fry, Florence Nightingale, 'Sister Dora', Caroline Chisholm i.a. Written in monotonously enthusiastic clichés for the child reader.

325   Lee, Sidney (ed.). *Dictionary of National Biography. Volume XLV Pereira – Pockrich.*

Smith and Elder, London.

Includes: Alice Perrers, Mary Peters, Emily Pfeiffer, Philippa of Hainault, Philippa of Lancaster, Katherine Philips, Catherine Phillips, Theresia Phillips, Joanna Picken, Ellen Pickering, Elizabeth Pigot, Harriet Pigott, Laetitia Pilkington, Mary Pilkington, Hester Piozzi (Mrs Thrale), Ann and Harriet Pitt, Mary Pix and Anne and Annabella Plumptre.

326 Lee, Sidney (ed.). *Dictionary of National Biography. Volume XLVI Pocock – Puckering.*

Smith and Elder, London.

Includes: Margaret Pole, Lady Emily Ponsonby, Sarah Ponsonby, Sophia Poole, Clara Pope, Elizabeth Pope, Jane Pope, Maria Pope, Anna Porter, Jane Porter, Mary Porter, Sarah Porter, Mrs Powell, Anne Pratt, Hannah Pritchard and Adelaide Procter.

327 Lee, Sidney (ed.). *Dictionary of National Biography. Volume XLVII Puckle – Reidford.*

Smith and Elder, London.

Includes: Dorothy Quillinan, Ann Radcliffe, Elizabeth Raffald, Elizabeth Rainforth, Ellen Ranyard, Hannah Rathbone, Martha Ray, Catherine Read and Clara Reeve.

328 Lee, Sidney (ed.). *Dictionary of National Biography. Volume XLVIII Reilly – Robins.*

Smith and Elder, London.

Includes: Mary Rich, Lady Penelope Rich, Charlotte Richardson, Louisa Rivarol and Mary Roberts.

1897

329 Dietrick, Ellen B. *Women in the Early Christian Ministry.* [American].

Alfred J. Ferris, Philadelphia.

Not seen.

330 Mundell, Frank. *Heroines of History.*

The Sunday School Union, London. Illustrated.

Includes Joan of Arc, Catherine Douglas, Lucy Hutchinson, Lady Rachel Russell and Flora Macdonald.

331 Mundell, Frank. *Heroines of Travel.*

The Sunday School Union, London. Illustrated.

Preface: 'Only within the last half-century have women engaged in travel on a large scale for its own sake. ... Since Mme Ida Pfeiffer quite a number of women have ventured into some of the least known countries of the world.' Includes Mme Pfeiffer, Isabella Bird, Mrs Gordon Cumming, Lady Brassey, Lady Baker, Lady Barker, Lady Florence Dixie, Miss Mena Muriel Dowie, Mrs French Sheldon, Geraldine Guinness and Mary Kingsley.

41. 'A Halt in the Desert' – frontispiece to Mundell's *Heroines of the Cross*, 1897.

332 Mundell, Frank. *Heroines of the Cross.*

The Sunday School Union, London. Illustrated.

Includes women missionaries, especially those martyred, e.g. Mrs Steward in China.

333 Vincent, Arthur (ed.). *Lives of Twelve Bad Women – Illustrations and Reviews of Feminine Turpitude set forth by impartial hands.*

T. Fisher Unwin, London. Illustrated.

Misogynist, prurient sequel to *Twelve Bad Men* (ed. Seccombe).

Comprises: Alice Perrers, d. 1400, Alice Arden executed 1551, 'Moll Cut-purse', Frances Howard, d. 1632, Barbara Villiers, d. 1709, Jenny Diver, executed 1741, Teresia Constantia Phillips, d. 1765,

Elizabeth Brownrigg, executed 1767, Elizabeth Canning, 'Impostor', executed 1773, Elizabeth Chudleigh, Duchess of Kingston, d. 1788, Mary Bateman, 'The Yorkshire Witch', d. 1809 and Mary Anne Clarke, d. 1852.

334   Brown, James D. and Stratton, S. *British Musical Biography – A Dictionary of Musical Artists, Authors and Composers born in Britain and its colonies.*

S. S. Stratton, Birmingham. 460 pp.

Preface: 'The authors have [desired] to present the true position of the British Empire in the world of Music. A country is musical only by the music it produces for itself not by what it takes from others. ... Therefore only what has been done by Britain's own sons and daughters is placed on record [here]. It is probable that in no other nation is there, at the present time, greater musical activity, creative or executive, than is to be witnessed in our own.'

Sources used include *Musical World, Dramatic and Musical Review, Musical Times, Musical Standard, Orchestral Times, British Musicians* and *Musical Herald.*

Includes Harriet Abrams, Susannah Cibber, Mary Gabriel, Elizabeth Masson, Christine Morison, Florence May, Caroline Norton, Lady Morgan, Clara Novello, Caroline Orger, Mary Paton, Liza Lehmann, Fanny Davies, Arabella Goddard, Elizabeth Mounsey, Mme Vestris, Anastasia Robinson, Ethel Smyth, Sophie Woolf and Marie Wurm. A fascinating, underused source, especially invaluable for those British women musicians, singers and instrumentalists who also composed before Ethel Smyth.

335   *Pratt, Edwin. *Pioneer Women in Victoria's Reign. Short Histories of Great Movements.*

George Newnes, London.

Indispensable chapters on 'Employments for Women', 'Emigration', 'The Higher Education of Women', 'Pioneer Women Doctors', 'Nursing', 'Poor Law Reform', 'Associations for Girls'. Includes: Mrs Wardroper, Matron of St Thomas' Hospital, Florence Lees, district nurse; Louisa Twining, workhouse reformer; Mrs Nassau Senior, befriender of workhouse girls; and Elizabeth Gilbert, blind activist for the blind, i.a. An important, underused source.

336 Gerard, Frances A. *Some fair Hibernians – being a supplementary volume to Some Celebrated Irish Beauties of the Last Century.*

Ward and Downey, London.

The author also wrote a biography of Angelica Kauffmann.

Includes Dorothy Jordan, Sarah Curran, Lady Blessington, Sidney Owenson (later Lady Morgan), Caroline Norton, Eliza O'Neill and Lola Montez.

337 Lee, Sidney (ed.). *Dictionary of National Biography. Volume XLIX Robinson – Russell.*

Smith and Elder, London.

Includes: Anastasia Robinson, Martha Robinson, Mary Robinson ('Perdita'), Amy Robsart, Regina Roche, Emma Romer, Isabella Romer, Margaret Roper, Christina Rossetti, Lucy Madox Rossetti, Maria Rossetti, Clara Rousby, Martha Routh, Frederica Rowan, Elizabeth Rowe, Mary Rowlandson, Susanna Rowson, Mary Rundall, Maria Rundell, Lady Elizabeth Russell, Lucy Russell (Countess of Bedford) and Lady Rachel Russell.

338 Lee, Sidney (ed.). *Dictionary of National Biography. Volume L Russen – Scobell.*

Smith and Elder, London.

Includes: Elizabeth Ryves, Maria Saffery, Catherine St Aubyn, Charlotte Sainton-Dolby, Florentia Sale, Lucy Sale-Barker, Eliza Salmon, Hester Santlow, Margaret Saunders, Alice Scarth, Mary Schimmelpenninck, Lady Charlotte Schreiber and Countess von der Schulenberg.

339 Lee, Sidney (ed.). *Dictionary of National Biography. Volume LI Scoffin – Sheares.*

Smith and Elder, London.

Includes: Lady Caroline Scott, Elizabeth Scott, Lady Harriet Scott, Sarah Scott, Catharine Sedley, Anne Seguin, Priscilla Sellon, Lavinia and Olivia Serres, Sarah Setchel, Anna Seward, Mary Sewell, Queen Sexburga, Saint Sexburga, Mrs Seymour, Catherine Grey Seymour, Eliza, Louisa and Mary Sharpe, Rolinda Sharples and Mary Postans Shaw.

340 Lee, Sidney (ed.). *Dictionary of National Biography. Volume LII Shearman – Smirke.*

Smith and Elder, London.

Includes: Anne Sheepshanks, Mary Shelley, Elizabeth Sheppard,

Caroline Sheridan, Elizabeth Sheridan, Frances Sheridan, Helen Sheridan (Dufferin), Martha Sherwood, Georgiana Shipley, Mother Shipton, Emily Shirreff, Jane Shore, Louisa and Margaret Shore, Harriet Siddons, Sarah Siddons, Jane Simpson, Catherine Sinclair and Lady Mary Slingsby.

1898

341 'Tytler, Sarah'. *Six Royal Ladies of the House of Hanover.*

Hutchinson and Co., London.

The wives of the four Georges and of William IV.

342 Mundell, Frank. *Heroines of the Faith.*

The Sunday School Union, London.

His final Sunday School prize offering. The cover shows young Margaret Wilson, Covenanter, executed by drowning in the Solway near Wigton. Includes only Protestant martyrs or persecuted Dissenters: Anne Askew, Margaret Baxter, Joyce Lewes, Alice Benden, Mary Dyer, Elizabeth Bunyan, Isabel Alison and Marion Hervey.

343 *Thayer, William M. *Women Who Win – or Making Things Happen.*

T. Nelson and Sons, London and New York.

The author also wrote *Men Who Win*.

Preface: 'There is no sex among souls ... it is soul-culture that God requires, which includes the development of physical and intellectual powers. ... Until within fifty years, men planned, legislated, and governed as if there were sex among souls. Out of this mistake grew manifold evils in social, intellectual, and even in religious life. ... [But] women are joint-partners now in making the world better. ... They make history. Their biographies are as really national history now as the biographies of the male sex. ... This volume [proves] that women are as able and bright as men ... and can become as great achievers for humanity and God.'

His Anglo-American roll-call includes: Elizabeth Fry, Harriet Beecher Stowe, Margaret Fuller, Jenny Lind, Dorothea Dix, Mary Somerville, Frances Power Cobbe, Mary Lyon, Mary Livermore, Louisa Alcott, Lucy Stone, Frances Willard and Clara Barton (co-founder of International and American Red Cross) – not remarking how very few of them also had children.

344 Lee, Sidney (ed.). *Dictionary of National Biography. Volume LIII Smith – Stanger.*

Smith and Elder, London.

Includes: Charlotte Smith, Elizabeth Smith, Lady Pleasance Smith, Harriet Smithson, Emily Smythe, Hannah Snell, Mary Somerville, Joanna Southcott, Caroline Southey, Elizabeth Soyer, Elizabeth Spence, Dorothy Spencer, Lily Spender and Maria Spilsbury.

345 Lee, Sidney (ed.). *Dictionary of National Biography. Volume LIV Stanhope – Stovin.*

Smith and Elder, London.

Includes: Lady Hester Stanhope, Lady Charlotte Stanley, Lady Henrietta Stanley, Venetia Stanley, Marianna Starke, Anne Steele, Catherine Stephens, Jane Stephens, Lady Catherine Stepney, Lady Maria Stewart-Mackenzie, Mary Stirling and Anna Storace.

346 Lee, Sidney (ed.). *Dictionary of National Biography. Volume LV Stow – Taylor.*

Smith and Elder, London.

Includes: Agnes Strickland, Jane Strickland, Lady Frances Stuart, Princess Maria Clementina Stuart, Lady Emmeline Stuart-Wortley, Lady Charlotte Sundon, Catherine Swynford, Marie Taglioni, Catherine Talbot, Elizabeth Talbot ('Bess of Hardwick'), Mary Anne Talbot, Baroness von Tautphoelus, Emily Taylor, Helen Taylor, Jane Taylor and Susannah Taylor.

347 Lee, Sidney (ed.). *Dictionary of National Biography. Volume LVI Teach – Tollet.*

Smith and Elder, London.

Includes: Dorothy Osborne Temple, Ann Thicknesse, Elizabeth Thomas, Katharine Thomson, Mary Thornycroft, Dorothea Thrupp, Mrs Thurmond, Mary Tighe, Teresa Titiens, Mary Toft, Katherine Tofts and Elizabeth Tollet.

1899

348 Garrison, W. L. Jr *et al. True Stories of Heroic Lives – Stirring Tales of Courage and Devotion of Men and Women of the Nineteenth Century, told for the most part by personal acquaintances and eye witnesses.*

Funk and Wagnalls, New York and London.

Anecdotes for children: subjects include heroines of the American Civil War, and of Cuba's independence struggle, as well as Florence Nightingale.

349   Chappell, Jennie. *Noble Workers.*

S. W. Partridge, London. New edition 1900 with portraits and illustrations.

Sketches of the lifework of Frances Willard, Agnes Weston, 'Sister Dora', Catherine Booth, Baroness Burdett Coutts, Lady Henry Somerset, Sarah Robinson, Mrs Fawcett and Mrs Gladstone.

A saccharine, largely Temperance volume in which Mrs Fawcett seems somewhat incongruous. Note this author's equally pious volume *Women Who Have Worked and Won* on Mrs Spurgeon, Emma Booth-Tucker, Frances Havergal and Pandita Ramabai published in 1903.

350   Richardson, Mrs Aubrey. *Famous Ladies of the English Court.*

Hutchinson and Co., London. Illustrated.

Preface wonders at the 'fearlessness and force of such women as Bess of Hardwick, Lady Anne Clifford and the Duchess of Marlborough'. Also includes Lady Mary Sidney, Countess of Pembroke, Penelope Rich and Lady Sarah Lennox.

351   Carey, Nouchette, Rosa. *Twelve Notable Good Women of the XIX Century.*

Hutchinson, London. Illustrated.

A preponderance of royals, especially Queen Victoria. Sentimentally Christian. Includes Elizabeth Fry, Florence Nightingale, Baroness Burdett Coutts, 'Sister Dora', Agnes Weston, Grace Darling, Lady Henry Somerset and Frances Havergal.

352   *Plarr, Victor. *Men and Women of the Time: A Dictionary of Contemporaries.*

George Routledge and Sons, London. 15th edition revised.

Note also the earlier editions: 1852, 1853, 1856, 1857, 1862, 1865, 1868, 1872, 1875, 1879, 1884, 1887, 1891, 1895.

Includes actresses, women educationalists, writers, singers, artists, social reformers, musicians, travellers and three women doctors. An underused source.

353   Lee, Sidney (ed.). *Dictionary of National Biography. Volume LVII Tom – Tytler.*

Smith and Elder, London.

Includes: Elizabeth Tomlins, Charlotte Tonna, Camilla Toulmin (Newton Crosland), Rebecca Travers, Abbess Letice Tredway, Melesina Trench, Sarah Trimmer, Frances Trollope, Theodosia

Trollope, Charlotte Tucker, Anne Turner, Mme Tussaud and Elizabeth Twining.

354   Lee, Sidney (ed.). *Dictionary of National Biography. Volume LVIII Tubaldini – Wakefield.*

Smith and Elder, London.

Includes: Fanny Umphelby, Mary Unwin, Saint Ursula, Charlotte Vandenhoff, Anne Vane, Lady Frances Vane, Esther Vanhomrigh ('Vanessa'), Anne Vaux, Margaret Veley, Susanna Verbruggen, Elizabeth Vesey, Lady Barbara Villiers ('Castlemain'), Elizabeth Villiers, Eva Violetti, Rosina Vokes, Joan Vokins and Priscilla Wakefield.

355   Lee, Sidney (ed.). *Dictionary of National Biography. Volume LVIX Wakeman – Watkins.*

Smith and Elder, London.

Includes: Abbess Walburga, Frances Waldegrave, Charlotte and Jane Waldie, Elizabeth Walker, Clementina Walkinshaw, Lady Eglantine Wallace, Lady Grace Wallace, Mrs Wallis, Amalie Wallmoden, Countess of Walsingham, Lucy Walter, Lady Elizabeth Wardlaw and Mary Warner.

356   Lee, Sidney (ed.). *Dictionary of National Biography. Volume LX Watson – Whewell.*

Smith and Elder, London.

Includes: Caroline Watson, Harriet Waylett, Mrs Webb, Augusta Webster, Mary Wells, Jane Wenham, Henrietta Wentworth, Saint Werburga, Mrs West, Jane West, Elizabeth Weston, Miss Wewitzer and Anne Wharton.

1900

357   Baring-Gould, S. *Virgin Saints and Martyrs.*

Hutchinson and Co., London.

Opinionated, racist and anti-Catholic work.

Includes: Blandina, Caecilia, Agnes, Febronia, Bridget, Hilda, Hildegarde of Bingen, Clara and Theresa of Avila: 'whose useless project it was to confine her fellows to moping in cells ... in compulsory idleness [influenced as she was by the Inquisition]. ... The Latin races seem doomed by God to go down, and His hand is manifestly extended to bless and lead on the great Anglo-Saxon race.' Ends with 'Sister Dora' of Walsall. Note also Agnes B. C. Dunbar, *A Dictionary of Saintly Women* (George Bell, 1904), with its scholarly bibliography.

358 Lee, Sidney (ed.). *Dictionary of National Biography. Volume LXI
     Whichcord – Williams.*

     Smith and Elder, London.

     Includes: Alice White, Elizabeth Whitlock, Leonora Wigan, Lady
     Jane Wilde, Anna Williams, Helen Maria Williams and Jane
     Williams.

359 Lee, Sidney (ed.). *Dictionary of National Biography. Volume LXII
     Williamson – Worden.*

     Smith and Elder, London.

     Includes: Mrs Wilson, Caroline Wilson, Harriette Wilson, Henrietta
     Wilson, Margaret Wilson, Mary Wilson, Saint Winefride, Catherine
     and Susanna Winkworth, Peg Woffington, Mrs Henry Wood, Mrs
     Woodham, Anne Woodroffe, Hannah Woolley and Emma Wor-
     boise.

360 Lee, Sidney (ed.). *Dictionary of National Biography. Volume LXII
     Wordsworth – Zuylestein.*

     Smith and Elder, London.

     Includes: Patience Wright, Lady Mary Wroth, Charlotte Wynn,
     Elizabeth Yates, Mary Ann Yates, Ann Yearsley and Elizabeth
     Younger.

1901

361 Denny, J. K. H. *Towards the Sunrising – A History of the work for the
     women of India done by women from England 1852–1900.*

     Marshall Bros., London and Zenana Bible and Medical Mission,
     London. Illustrated with many photographs.

     Note the Appendix listing all British women medical missionaries
     since 1852.

362 Lee, Sidney (ed.). *Dictionary of National Biography Supplement.
     Abbot – Childers.*

     Smith and Elder, London.

     Includes: Mrs Alexander, Lady Marian Alford, Mary Anning,
     Isabella Banks, Lydia Becker, Mathilde Blind, Barbara Leigh Smith
     Bodichon, Catherine Booth, Annie Brassey, Eleanor Bufton, Isabel
     Burton, Julia Byrne, Ada Cavendish and Elizabeth Charles.

363 Lee, Sidney (ed.). *Dictionary of National Biography Supplement.
     Chippendale – Hoste.*

     Smith and Elder, London.

Includes: Mary Chippendale, Mary Cowden Clarke, Anne Jemima Clough, Eliza Cook, Julia Corner, Pauline Craven, Augusta Drane, Lady Eastlake, Amelia Edwards, Helena Faucit, Lydia Foote and Lady Mary Hardy.

364 Lee, Sidney (ed.). *Dictionary of National Biography Supplement. How – Woodward.*

Smith and Elder, London.

Includes: Margaret Hungerford, Jean Ingelow, Annie Ireland, Lady Catherine Jackson, Mary Keeley, Fanny Kemble, Mary Kingsley, Carlotta and Rosa Leclercq, Eliza Lynn Linton, Anne Manning, Margaret the Maid of Norway, Emma Marshall, Margaret Oliphant, Amy Sedgwick, Margaret Stokes, Anna Swanwick, Queen Victoria and Mary Ward.

42. St Joan leading a Suffrage march in London, June 1911.

EPILOGUE

1907–8

365 Hamilton, Cicely. *A Pageant of Great Women.*

The Suffrage Shop, London. Illustrated.

1910 edition held in the Fawcett Library.

Agitprop street-theatre for the British Women's Suffrage Movement, the original production designed by Edith Craig. Contemporary photographs show Boadicea, Hilda of Whitby, Joan of Arc, Nance Oldfield, Christian Davies, Elizabeth Fry, Charlotte Brontë, Florence Nightingale, Rosa Bonheur and others taking to the streets of London, or performing in private houses and theatres, in order to support The Cause.

43. Mrs Despard as Abbess Hilda of Whitby and Edith Craig as the painter Rosa Bonheur, from Hamilton's *Pageant of Great Women*, 1908. Fawcett Library, London Guildhall University.

A Pageant of Great Women

ARRANGED BY EDITH CRAIG

Assistant Stage Manager: MR. A. G. FORDE

Music arranged by MR. J. M. CAPEL

JUSTICE	LADY GROVE
PREJUDICE	MR. KENYON MUSGROVE
WOMAN	MISS ADELINE BOURNE

THE LEARNED WOMEN

Hypatia	MISS ELAINE INESCOURT
St. Teresa	MISS ADA POTTER
Lady Jane Grey	MISS DOROTHY FINNEY
Madame de Stael	MISS FRANCES VANE
Madame Roland	MISS MAUDE HOFFMAN
Madame de Scudéry	MISS NORA ROYSTON
Jane Austen	MISS WINIFRED MAYO
George Sand	MISS MARY WEBB
Caroline Herschell	MISS BRINETA BROWNE
Madame Curie	MISS MARGARET MARSHALL
Graduate	MISS MAUDE BUCHANAN

THE ARTISTS

Sappho	MISS EVA BALFOUR
Vittoria Colonna	MISS GWENDOLINE BISHOP
Angelica Kauffmann	MISS ROSE MATHEWS
Vigée le Brun	MISS MARGARET HALSTAN
Rosa Bonheur	MISS EDITH CRAIG
Margaret van Eyck	MISS IRENE ROSS
Nance Oldfield	MISS ELLEN TERRY

THE SAINTLY WOMEN

St. Hilda	MISS MADELINE ROBERTS
Elizabeth Fry	MISS JOY CHATWYN
Elizabeth of Hungary	MISS GWLADYS MORRIS
Catherine of Siena	MRS. MADELINE LUCETTE RYLEY

THE HEROIC WOMEN

Charlotte Corday	MRS. BROWN POTTER
Flora Macdonald	MISS MONA HARRISON
Kate Barlass	MISS EVELYN HAMMILL
Grace Darling	MISS BARBARA AYRTON

THE RULERS

Victoria	MISS ANGELA HUBBARD
Elizabeth	MISS JANETTE STEER
Zenobia	MISS NELLA POWYS
Philippa	MRS. SAM SOTHERN
Deborah	MISS EDYTH OLIVE
Isabella	MISS GRANVILLE
Catherine the Great	MISS SUZANNE SHELDON
Tsze-Hsi-An	MISS VIOLA FINNEY

THE WARRIORS

Joan of Arc	MISS PAULINE CHASE
Boadicea	MISS ELIZABETH KIRBY
Agnes of Dunbar	MISS FRANCES WETHERALL
Emilie Plater	MISS MIRIAM LEWES
Rance of Jhansi	MUNCI CAPEL
Maid of Saragossa	MISS VERA COBURN
Christian Davies	MISS CICELY HAMILTON
Hannah Snell	MISS CHRISTOPHER ST. JOHN
Mary Ann Talbot	MRS. R. RATHBONE
Florence Nightingale	MISS MARION TERRY

43. Cast-list of *A Pageant of Great Women*.

Category Index

References are to item numbers not page numbers.
Note: for Gillian Fenwick's categories of the individual women listed in the first *DNB*, see her *Women in the Dictionary of National Biography* (1994).

Actresses   26, 33, 44, 46, 50, 58, 62, 72, 79, 97, 98, 101, 103, 174, 196, 212, 219, 252, 352
Adventurers, including soldiers and pirates   72, 73a, 88, 203, 298
American women   130, 175, 219a, 223, 301, 343, 348
Anglican women   32, 55, 93, 95
Aristocrats, including land-owning women   43, 48, 65, 117, 149, 152, 182, 197, 200, 236, 350
Artists   23, 43, 75, 86, 145, 184, 192, 255, 322, 352

Calvinists   115, 127, 219a, 342
Catholics   3, 31, 34, 35, 42, 128, 181, 228, 242, 244, 250, 251, 320, 357
Classical women of antiquity   9, 22, 68b, 102, 111a, 122, 133
Composers   179, 237, 321, 334
Criminals   72, 73a, 81, 88, 333

Doctors (*see also* Medical missionaries)   208, 234, 293, 335, 352

Educationalists/teachers (*see also* Missionaries)   190, 208, 209, 293, 322, 335, 352, 361
Eighteenth-century women   32, 37, 39, 50, 51, 53, 54, 59, 62, 66, 68b, 79, 90, 91, 97, 98, 113, 117, 124, 153, 161, 174, 184, 192, 204, 219, 237, 334

Feminists   170, 175, 223, 322
Freethinkers/'heretics'   6, 266
Frenchwomen   57, 76, 124, 128, 138, 157, 182
Friends   108, 142

Girls   12, 13, 15, 67, 70, 129, 147, 162, 173, 195, 207, 215, 243
Gypsies   72, 73a, 88

Heroines   9, 106, 118, 133, 150, 151, 167, 171, 191, 201, 210, 293, 323, 324, 330, 331, 332, 342, 348

Indian women   111a, 189, 190, 279
Irishwomen   90, 91, 196, 199, 202, 287, 336

Jewish women, Old Testament   5, 9, 21, 111a, 114, 133

Learned women   1, 8, 22, 38, 41, 44, 51, 59, 63, 68b, 72, 103, 113, 121, 194, 195, 205

Martyrs   2, 13, 15, 34, 42, 64, 111a, 128, 171, 181, 219a, 251, 342, 357
Mediaeval women   3, 35, 42, 110a, 128, 152, 181, 227, 242, 251, 320
Medical missionaries   130, 208, 234, 293, 361
Methodists   99, 265
Missionaries   130, 190, 208, 209, 210, 264, 293, 315, 322, 332
Mistresses   11, 44, 48, 72, 168, 333
Mothers   119, 144
Musicians   53, 54, 96, 204, 237, 256, 300, 322, 334, 352

Nineteenth-century women   90, 97, 98, 132, 156, 159, 161, 170, 174, 175, 177, 183, 184, 190, 192, 204, 210, 221, 222, 223, 226, 229, 234, 237, 269, 293, 294, 296, 300, 301, 315, 334, 335, 343, 349, 351, 352, 361

Name Index

GILBERT, Elizabeth Philippa, activist for the blind *275*, 335
GILCHRIST, Anne, biographer of Mary Lamb *275*
GILLIES, Margaret, artist *275*
+ **GILLILAND, T.** 79
+ **GILLOW, J.** 228
GIRLING, Mary Anne, Messianic prophetess *275*
GISBORNE, Maria, friend of Shelley *275*
GLADSTONE, Mrs 229, 349
GLASSE, Hannah, cookery writer *275*
GLAUBER, Diana 86
GLOVER, Jean, poet *276*
GLOVER, Julia, actress 212, 252, *276*
GLYN, Isabella, actress *276*
GOBAT, Mrs 209, 264
GODDARD, Arabella 334
GODELEVA, Saint 320
GODEWYCK, Margaret 86
GODIVA, or GODGIFU, Lady 16, *276*
GODOLPHIN, Margaret 235, *276*
GODWIN, Catherine, poet *276*
GODWIN, Mary Wollstonecraft xv, 66, 68b, 72, 73, 74, 75, 87, 103, 113, 130, 266, *276*
GOLDIE, Mg. 242
GOLDSMID, Anna, philanthropist *276*
GOLDSMITH, Sarah 29
GOMEZ, Louisa 190
GONZAGA sisters 45, 47, 87
GOODAL, Mrs 115
GOODALL, Charlotte, actress *276*
GOODFELLOW, Anne 7
GORDON, Elizabeth, Duchess of 218, *276*
GORDON, Lady Henrietta *276*
GORDON, Jane, Duchess of 149, *276*
GORDON, Lucie Duff, traveller 253, *276*, 307
GORE, Catherine, writer *276*
GOREH, Ellen Lakshmi 292
GOSSE, Emily, religious writer *276*
GOUGES, Olympe de 130

GOULD, John 86
GOURNAY, Marie de Jars 45, 47, 57, 75, 87, 157
GOWDIE, Isobel 140
GRACE, Mary, artist *276*
GRADDON, Miss, singer *276*
GRAHAM, Clementina, writer *276*
GRAHAM, Elizabeth 19
GRAHAM, Janet, poet *276*
GRAHAM-STIRLING, Miss 198
GRAHN, Theodora 73a
+ **GRANGER, James** 48, 153
GRANT, Anne, of Laggan 121, 164, 169, *276*
GRANT, Elizabeth, writer *276*
GRAY, Maria, conchologist *277*
GREBIL, Agnes 2
GREEN, Eliza, poet *277*
+ **GREEN, Mary Ann Everett** 123, *277*
GREENE, Anne, criminal *277*
GREENLIEF, Ellen 7
GREENWELL, Dora, writer *277*, 292
GREY, Lady Catherine 117, 173, *339*
GREY, Elizabeth, Countess of Kent, writer *277*
GREY, Lady Jane xv, 1, 15, 24, 36, 38, 45, 55, 65, 87, 89, 93, 105, 107, 133, 136, 141, 171, 173, 215, 220, *263*
GREY, Maria, pioneer educationalist 299
GREY, Lady Mary 173, *290*
GRIERSON, Constantia 38, 44, 52, 91, 196, 199, 202, *277*
GRIERSON, Julia 196
GRIFFITH, Elizabeth, writer 87, *277*
GRIFFITH, Frederic 321
GRIFFITHS, Ann, hymn writer *277*
GRIMKÉ, Sarah and Angelina 175
GRIMSTON, Elizabeth, writer *277*
GRISI, Mme Carlotta 159, 204
GROTE, Harriet, biographer *277*
GROVES, G. 204
GRUNDY, Isobel xvi
GUINNESS, Geraldine 331
GUIZOT, Mme 169
GUNDRADA, Lady de Warenne *277*